MW01193687

"*Cradled in Hope* of miscarriage and Ashley's book is a heartfelt reminder that healing and hope are found in His embrace. This tender guide is for anyone seeking peace while they grieve. It is a great joy to know resources, such as this must-read book, exist to care for women."

Sarah Philpott, bestselling author of books, including *Loved Baby: 31 Devotions Helping You Grieve and Cherish Your Child After Pregnancy Loss*

"Beautifully pointing the hurting heart to the hope of the Gospel, Ashley Opliger's *Cradled in Hope* gently (yet powerfully) carries the reader toward the promise of healing Jesus offers and His promised presence in the midst of such a painful season. I experienced my own miscarriages over fifteen years ago, and I still found Ashley's inspired words deeply moving. *Cradled in Hope* is a gift to those who are ready to trust Jesus to heal their hearts as He holds their babies in Heaven, and it is a much-needed resource for the body of Christ."

Becky Thompson, *USA TODAY* bestselling author

"*Cradled in Hope* is a compassionate and faith-filled resource for anyone grieving miscarriage, stillbirth, or infant loss. Ashley Opliger not only tenderly weaves encouragement and biblical hope into each page, but also provides practical guidance for navigating grief. This book is a comforting companion, reminding readers that even in sorrow, there is hope."

Julie Busler, Bible teacher, speaker, and author of *Joyful Sorrow* and *Hopeful Sorrow*

"Ashley Opliger meets grieving mothers in the darkness of pregnancy and infant loss and shines the light of hope. She approaches the heartbreaking and traumatic realities of loss with candor while boldly proclaiming Jesus. *Cradled in Hope* weaves together hurt and healing in a profoundly beautiful way."

Jenny Albers, author of *Courageously Expecting: 30 Days of Encouragement for Pregnancy After Loss*

"*Cradled in Hope* is a tender, truth-filled guide for every mother who has faced the unbearable sorrow of losing a baby. With deep compassion and unwavering faith, Ashley invites grieving moms into a sacred space where their pain is acknowledged, their babies are remembered, and their hearts are gently led to Jesus. She writes like a trusted friend sitting beside you—listening, understanding, and reminding you that while grief is heavy, hope is always within reach. As someone who has walked the painful road of baby loss, I am profoundly grateful for this book. It is a gift to any mother searching for comfort, a firm foundation of faith, and the promise that she is not alone. Ashley's words are a light in the darkness, pointing every hurting heart to the One who cradles both us and our babies in His arms."

Jennie Parks, executive director of Hope Mommies

"Ashley Opliger is the compassionate friend we all need in grief—holding your hand with understanding and care while continually pointing to the unshakable hope we have in Christ. This book is a beautiful biblical companion, filled with truth, comfort, and hope on every page."

Kristin Hernandez, host of the *Hope Mommies Podcast* and author of *Sunlight in December: A Mother's Story of Finding the Goodness of God in the Storm of Grief*

Cradled
in **Hope**

Cradled *in* Hope

TRUSTING JESUS TO HEAL YOUR HEART
AS HE HOLDS YOUR BABY IN HEAVEN–

A BIBLICAL GUIDE FOR GRIEVING
MISCARRIAGE, STILLBIRTH, AND INFANT LOSS

ashley opliger

BETHANYHOUSE
a division of Baker Publishing Group
Minneapolis, Minnesota

Published by Bethany House Publishers
Minneapolis, Minnesota
BethanyHouse.com

Bethany House Publishers is a division of
Baker Publishing Group, Grand Rapids, Michigan

Printed in the United States of America

Library of Congress Cataloging-in-Publication Data
Names: Opliger, Ashley, author.
Title: Cradled in hope : trusting Jesus to heal your heart as he holds your
   baby in heaven : a biblical guide for grieving miscarriage, stillbirth,
   and infant loss / Ashley Opliger.
Description: Minneapolis, Minnesota : Bethany House Publishers, a division
   of Baker Publishing Group, [2025] | Includes bibliographical references.
Identifiers: LCCN 2024054642 | ISBN 9780764244346 (paperback) | ISBN
   9780764245091 (casebound) | ISBN 9781493450862 (ebook)
Subjects: LCSH: Consolation. | Miscarriage—Religious
   Aspects—Christianity. | Stillbirth—Religious aspects—Christianity. |
   Premature infants—Death—Religious aspects—Christianity. |
   Bereavement—Religious aspects—Christianity.
Classification: LCC BV4907 .O65 2025 | DDC 248.8/66—dc23/eng/20250109
LC record available at https://lccn.loc.gov/2024054642

The author is not a licensed counselor or medical provider. This publication is intended to provide helpful and informative material on the subjects addressed. Readers should consult their personal health professionals before adopting any of the suggestions in this book or drawing inferences from it. The author and publisher expressly disclaim responsibility for any adverse effects arising from the use or application of the information contained in this book.

The author includes quotations from other people to support the ideas and theology shared in *Cradled in Hope*. Though the author stands by these quotes, the use of another person's quote(s) is not an endorsement of all their content and views, whether shared in the past or future.

Cover design by Dan Pitts
Cover illustration by Ellie Tilev

The author is represented by the literary agency of The Blythe Daniel Agency, Inc.

Baker Publishing Group publications use paper produced from sustainable forestry practices and postconsumer waste whenever possible.

25 26 27 28 29 30 31   7 6 5 4 3 2 1

To _____

In Loving Memory of

_____

Heaven Date

_____

From _____

For Bridget

You changed my life more than any other person on this earth. I love you more than my heart can hold. I thank God every day for choosing me to be your mommy. It is the greatest blessing and honor of my life. I hope I have made you and our Heavenly Father proud with what I've done in your memory. I can't wait to gaze upon your precious face and explore Heaven with you for eternity. Until

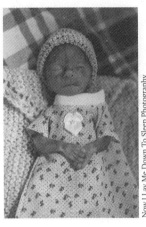

Now I Lay Me Down To Sleep Photography

then, I know Jesus cradles you in His arms, and there's no better place to be. My sweet and strong girl, I'll see you again soon. Love, Mommy

To Jesus

My words will fall short of giving You the glory You deserve. You are worthy of all my praise and honor. You are the reason I wrote this book. You lifted me from the pit of despair, healed my heart, and restored my joy. Your death and Resurrection sealed my salvation and gave me the greatest hope: to spend eternity with You in Heaven. Because of You, I will see Bridget again! I will never be able to thank You enough for what You've done for me. I pray my book is pleasing to You and points all who read it to You, my Savior, my Friend, my King. I love You from the depths of my soul and long to dwell in Your House forever. Until then, I will serve You and eagerly await Your return.

In Loving Memory of My Dad, Steven Richard Golik "SRG"

Dad, you were the first man I ever loved. Your consistent presence and unconditional love throughout my life have made it easy for me to believe in a good and loving Heavenly Father. You have always been there for me, helping me through both the happy and hard chapters of my life.

Jessica Noelle Photography

You always believed in me and supported my dreams. In fact, your investment in my taking a book proposal course was the catalyst that pushed me to write *Cradled in Hope*. You were so excited to read my book (even telling me you planned to buy your own copy). Though you won't be able to read it on earth, I believe God has allowed you to see it from Heaven.

Our earthly relationship started and ended with us looking into each other's eyes (the windows to our souls). Growing up, you always told me the story about the first time you held me when I was born (in 1987). Minutes after I was delivered, the nurses swaddled me and handed me to you, and I stared lovingly into your eyes for several minutes without crying. It was as if I knew you were my daddy. We've been bonded ever since.

We had a full-circle moment on the day you died at the hands of a drunk driver (in 2024) as I looked deep into your ocean-blue eyes and said my earthly good-byes. On that same day, you opened your eyes in Heaven to see the face of Jesus and your precious granddaughter, Bridget. As you said in the poem you wrote after she was born into Heaven (in 2014), your first embrace with her was a Heavenly embrace.

And just like the day you held me for the first time, you held Bridget for the first time and looked into her eyes—and she knew it was you. She knew it was you. I love you, Dad. I always have, and I always will. I thank Jesus for the hope of the coming Resurrection. Because of Him, the sting of death will not last forever, and I will surely look into your eyes again.

SRG, I dedicate my book to you.

Love you forever,
Ashley

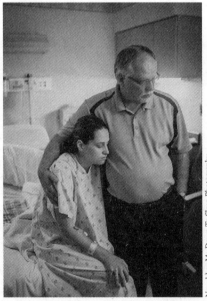

Now I Lay Me Down To Sleep Photography

Our First Embrace

A Poem Written by Steve Golik, Bridget's Grampy (October 2014)

In the spring, I was conceived in love and redemption
I knew nothing of earthly affairs or concerns
I felt the instant connection of parental love and an
environment of family
But one thing I did not know, is that our first embrace
would be a Heavenly embrace

Over the summer, there was a dramatic turn of events
For reasons only known to our God
My mommy and I fought together, summoning all the
courage we could
But one thing I did not know, is that our first embrace
would be a Heavenly embrace

On a fall morning in October, my earthly mission was
not revealed
My family loved me and dressed me like an angel, sent
me on to my next calling
I will wait patiently for all of you!
But one thing I know for sure, is that our first embrace
will be a Heavenly embrace!

To learn more about my dad's life and legacy, visit BridgetsCradles.com/Grampy. There, you will find a video of me reading his eulogy at his memorial service, as well as a video of him playing a song he composed on guitar for Bridget after she went to Heaven. He lovingly titled the song "Bridget's Ballad."

Now I Lay Me Down To Sleep Photography

Contents

Preface

HANDS

Look down at your hands. Have you considered how much they have metaphorically "witnessed"? Oh, they have endured something so traumatic.

No mother's hands should have to flush the toilet, wondering whether or not the swirling pool of blood contained her baby's remains. No mother's hands should have to feel the coldness of her dead baby's skin. No mother's hands should have to close her baby's casket or hold her baby's urn.

But these same hands also experienced something *sacred*: motherhood. Yours are the hands that held the pregnancy test stick when you jumped for joy at the news of your baby's life. Yours are the hands that rubbed your growing belly as you talked to your sweet baby nestled inside.

Your hands drove you to each doctor's appointment, checked your pregnancy app to see the size of your baby each week, and popped your prenatal vitamins into your mouth each morning (even though they made you sick). Yours are the hands of a loving and devoted mother.

For those of you who delivered and held your baby, your hands *touched* God's most precious creation. Your hands cradled your sweet baby in your arms, or maybe your tiny baby fit perfectly in the palm of your hand. Your fingers softly caressed their head and unclenched their tiny fist to fit your finger under theirs.

They are the hands that did the impossible task of packing up your hospital bag and going home without your baby. They are the hands that wiped countless tears from your cheeks. They are the hands that dialed the number to the funeral home, typed your baby's obituary, and placed flowers on their grave. They are the hands now empty. But, oh, what strong hands you have, momma.

I do not take lightly the fact that your hands are now holding my book. Look at how far you have come. Here you are, reading a biblical book on grief, committed to walking with Jesus through your pain. I am so proud of you! I can't explain how incredibly honored I am that you chose *my* hands to be the ones you trusted to hold on this journey.

Before we embark together, I'd like to share more about my hands, which have spent countless hours folded in prayer and thumbing through God's Word to write this book for you. I meticulously crafted each sentence and pored over every paragraph to share practical wisdom and rich theology to guide you into a closer relationship with Christ in the midst of your pain.

However, I must offer a disclaimer: I am not a licensed counselor or mental health professional. My hands do not hold "official" credentials to write this book, but they *have* held my precious thirteen-ounce daughter, Bridget, who was born into Heaven at twenty-four weeks in 2014. After her birth, God led my hands to start and lead a nationwide nonprofit in her memory called Bridget's Cradles.

Our ministry donates small knit and crocheted cradles to hospitals in all fifty states to hold stillborn babies born into Heaven in the second trimester of pregnancy. Maybe you are reading this book because you've held your baby in one of our cradles. If so, I'm so sorry you had a need for one. But I'm grateful that you had a dignifying way to hold your baby. You and I now share a special connection, and I hope you reach out to share your baby's story with me.

My hands hold the hands—both literally and figuratively—of dozens of grieving moms as I lead Christ-centered support groups online and in person at our headquarters in Kansas. My hands also hold a microphone as I host a Gospel-focused podcast for grieving moms that is also called *Cradled in Hope*. In addition, each year on October 15, Pregnancy and Infant Loss Remembrance Day, my hands hold a candle in memory of our babies in Heaven at an event we orchestrate called Wave of Light.

But before I started Bridget's Cradles, my hands received a master's degree in speech-language pathology from Wichita State University. I practiced for several years at various outpatient clinics and a school for the deaf, where my hands used sign language to teach students with hearing loss how to speak.

Several months after Bridget was born, God asked me to resign from my career to serve full-time with Bridget's Cradles. But more important than anything I've done in the past or do in the present is the fact that my hands are surrendered to Jesus. I am a fully devoted follower of Christ, and I love Him with all my heart.

But even though I am filled with His Holy Spirit, *my hands* and *this book* do not hold the power to heal your broken heart or give you what you so desperately long for—to be reunited with your baby. There is, however, a Man with *nail-scarred hands* who has the power to resurrect your baby and offer you eternity together in Heaven. He is holding your baby in Heaven now and desires to heal your heart on earth too.

Jesus is the One I want you to meet as you read my words on these pages. So, momma, place your weary hand in mine, and let's hold Jesus' hand together.

How to Read
Cradled in Hope

Flip back to the table of contents. You'll notice that each chapter has a title and a subtitle. The chapter title focuses on the **hope or truth** I want to impart to you, whereas the subtitle addresses the **emotion or struggle** you may be facing in your grief.

I structured the chapters to intentionally move you from pain to purpose and from heartbreak to hope. Though all the chapters contain practical wisdom, the beginning chapters are a bit heavier in theology in order to set the biblical foundation for the book. However, feel free to jump to specific chapters if you are struggling with a particular aspect of grief or would like to revisit chapters of interest.

For example, skip to chapter 5 if you want to learn more about what it's like for our babies to live in the glory of Heaven, or chapter 7 if you're struggling with blaming yourself for your loss. Go to chapter 8 if you're dealing with friends or family members who say hurtful things (or maybe say nothing at all), or chapter 10 if you're experiencing anxiety or panic attacks due to unwelcome triggers.

At the end of each chapter, you'll find the following four sections:

Prayers to Heaven: A prayer for you to lift up to God, the Creator of Heaven and earth, and His Son, Jesus, who sits at His right hand in Heaven. Each prayer allows you to connect with Him and seek His guidance in your grief.

Truth to Cling To: Additional Bible verses not previously shared in the chapter for further study. These passages align with the chapter's main ideas and are intended to give you real-time hope from God's Word.

Time with Jesus: Journal prompts that encourage you to reflect on your grief, faith, and journey with Jesus. The questions will lead you into a personal prayer time with the Lord. You can write your answers in your own journal or in the free, downloadable *Cradled in Hope (CIH) Guided Journal* (see details below).

Healing Steps: Action items to consider completing before reading the next chapter. You will find practical ways to honor your baby, process your grief, and put your faith into action. It's okay to come back to them at a later time if you desire to keep moving forward in the book.

• • • FREE *CRADLED IN HOPE* GUIDED JOURNAL • • •

Go to AshleyOpliger.com/Journal and download the free *Cradled in Hope (CIH) Guided Journal*. You can print the PDF or fill it out on your computer.

The *CIH Guided Journal* is a companion guide designed to accompany you on your healing journey with Jesus. It features the **Prayers to Heaven** written in the first person, making your prayers more intimate.

It also includes the **Truth to Cling To** full Bible verses typed out, **Time with Jesus** prompts with room for journaling, and **Healing Steps** in a convenient checklist format. Additionally, it provides links to other hope-filled resources from Bridget's Cradles, including our e-book, *Memorial Ideas for a Baby in Heaven.* This free PDF provides ways to honor your baby in your heart and home.

• • • A DOOR TO HOPE AND HEALING • • •

The book you're holding is more than just a book. I want it to be more like a door: Opening it leads you first to Jesus and second to an entire community of women ready to walk this journey with you. *Cradled in Hope* is designed to connect you with Bridget's Cradles' ministry and our community of Christ-centered support.

We host monthly support groups (often led by me), release Gospel-focused podcast episodes, and share hope-filled quotes and Scripture on our social media pages (@BridgetsCradles and @CradledinHope on Facebook and Instagram). For moms who attend our support groups, we send special cards and gifts on their baby's important milestones, such as their due date and Heaven Day.

Visit BridgetsCradles.com for more information. You can also find more details about our digital support group, Hope Online, and our *Cradled in Hope* podcast in the back of this book.

Introduction

Hugs at the Door

WHEN YOU NEED A FRIEND

Brothers and sisters, we do not want you to be uninformed about those who sleep in death, so that you do not grieve like the rest of mankind, who have no hope. For we believe that Jesus died and rose again, and so we believe that God will bring with Jesus those who have fallen asleep in him.

1 Thessalonians 4:13–14

Dear momma,

Oh, how I wish you did not need my book! My heart aches that you know the indescribable pain of losing a baby.[1] I never would have imagined I'd write a book about pregnancy and infant loss, and I'm sure you never expected to read one. But my entire life

---

1. I wrote this book using *baby* in the singular form to avoid writing *baby(ies)* with the added parentheses. This will make it easier to read, but I want to acknowledge and be sensitive to the many moms who sadly have multiple babies in Heaven. When you see *baby*, please know I am referring to *each baby* you have in Heaven.

changed when my daughter, Bridget Faith, was born into Heaven at 24 weeks on October 22, 2014.

I know your life has changed too. I wish we could have met another way, without sharing this mutual heartache. No mother wants to be in this club, but here we are—two mommas missing our babies and wondering how we will live without them. I wish we could be together in person, not separated by these pages, but I trust God has us where we are supposed to be.

I believe God had me write this book for you and purposefully placed it in your hands. As you read *Cradled in Hope*, you'll notice my writing style is to "go deep fast"—to be extra vulnerable in the personal stories I share and to dive into rich theology of the Bible. I do this so that we can know God and His Word better and practically apply it to our grief.

My friends would say I take this same approach to friendships in real life. It is simply how God made me. Though I don't know your name yet, I have prayed many prayers and cried many tears for you. I hope I can become a close friend to you, even if it's through ink on a page. So, friend, will you meet with me for a while?

• • • WELCOME TO KECHI • • •

I want to invite you to a small town in my home state of Kansas called Kechi. It's a quaint town located north of Wichita, the largest city in our state. Kechi has a population of two thousand and has one four-way stop on the main street, Kechi Road.

If you've ever taken a road trip through small-town America, you've probably driven through a town like this. It has one park, a gas station, and no chain restaurants or stores. Here you'll find a home-turned-quilt shop, an old playhouse, and a glass-blowing studio. It's a creative town with ma-and-pa shops specializing in arts and crafts and homemade knickknacks.

On Kechi Road sits your neighborly post office, where the three loyal staff members know every customer by name. People are friendly here, and the pace is slower. A minute's drive from the post office takes you over the railroad tracks and past some horse stables to a building resembling a barn.

The building's metal exterior walls are painted blue above gray stone that wraps around its base. It boasts a white tin roof and porch columns with modern farmhouse appeal. Four windows let in light that illuminates the interior, a cozy room in calming pastel colors.

Can you picture it? I want you to imagine meeting me in this space. I know you're wondering why I'm inviting you *here*, of all places. Well, because this Little Blue Barn is home to Bridget's Cradles headquarters, the ministry my husband and I founded in memory of our daughter, Bridget. I've welcomed many grieving moms here and sat with them face-to-face and heart-to-heart. This place has been their healing home, and I want it to be yours too.

In the Little Blue Barn, it's safe to say your baby's name and share your hurts, fears, and doubts. You can cry, ask why, and bring your pain and sadness. Here you can grieve, real and raw, and be vulnerable with your heart. It's your sacred space to re-member, reflect, and dream. Yes, it's even okay to laugh and feel joy here.

• • • COME AS YOU ARE • • •

There is no need to dress up or wear makeup. You don't need to impress anyone. Sweatpants and T-shirts are the dress code. I am in comfy clothes myself. I'm just here to be your friend.

You don't need to be at a specific place in your grief or feel a certain way about God. No sorrow is too fresh or too far out for you to come. Your grief is welcome here. Put your hair up in a messy bun or ponytail and come as you are. It's just going to be you, me, and Jesus.

Imagine that you pull up to the Little Blue Barn, park your car, and sigh, "Okay, here I am. I don't know what to expect, but I'm showing up." I know it can feel overwhelming to attend a support group or counseling session, or meet another bereaved mom for the first time.

Even reading a book about grief and opening yourself up to your pain and the process of healing can be scary. But here you are. You've shown up. I am so proud of you for the courage and bravery it took to get this far. You are one strong momma.

You walk up to our front door and ring the doorbell. I open the door and greet you with a hug. I know not everyone is a hugger like I am, but I want to show you how much I care. You need it, and it's okay to let your walls down to receive it.

I'd let your tears fall on my shoulder, and I'd be present with you in your pain. You wouldn't hear me extend platitudes or religious clichés, such as *Everything happens for a reason. God needed another angel. Your baby was too beautiful for earth. You should be grateful for your other children. You're still young and can try again.*

I know these well-intended statements from others cause you to hurt so much more. I wouldn't minimize your grief or attempt to justify your loss. I know there are no words to take your pain away, so I'd simply say *I'm so very sorry for your loss* and *I'm here for you.*

I would then show you around the cozy thousand-square-foot room, pointing out the beautiful floral mural of Psalm 139 (the "fearfully and wonderfully made" verse). My friend hand painted it in memory of her daughter in Heaven. I would then share about my daughter and the ministry operations and support groups that happen here.

We would sit in two comfy gray chairs next to each other, separated by a cute table with gold legs that holds my Bible and a pretty lamb's ear plant. Kleenexes sit close by, and string lights softly glow overhead in the open rafters. Worship music softly plays in the background. I would then ask to hear your baby's life story, as I know you're missing them more than your heart can stand.

• • • YOUR BABY'S STORY MATTERS • • •

You'd start from the beginning. You'd share with me how long it took you to conceive your baby after struggling with infertility for years or how this pregnancy was a surprise that came at an unexpected but needed time.

You'd tell me about your pregnancy, including when you first saw those two pink lines and how you told your friends and family. We'd talk about whether you had a gender reveal party and the theme you picked for your baby's nursery.

Then, with tears in your eyes, you'd tell me how many weeks along you were or how old your baby was when the unthinkable happened. You'd describe the horrible sequence of events that led to the devastating day the doctor told you that your baby no longer had a heartbeat.

Or maybe your baby had medical complications diagnosed in utero, and doctors predicted they wouldn't live past birth. Perhaps you were shocked that after a healthy pregnancy, when your baby was born, instead of hearing the shrill cry of a newborn, silence filled the delivery room. Or, in a mother's worst nightmare, you put your infant down for a nap, and your baby never woke up.

I'd listen intently to every detail you were comfortable sharing with me, and my heart would ache with yours. You'd tell me your baby's name, and I'd comment on how much I love the name you chose. You'd then explain the excruciating moments and days following your baby's death. We'd cry together as you recounted the sorrowful days of planning your baby's burial or cremation and their funeral.

If you had pictures of your sweet baby, you'd pull those up on your phone. I'd look in awe at his or her adorable little features, so fearfully and wonderfully made. We'd talk about his long fingers or her cute button nose. You'd mention the special blanket or cradle wrapping your baby in love and how much it meant to you.

If your loss was early, we'd grieve over the fact that you never got the chance to see your baby's face or tell people you were pregnant. We would talk about your miscarriage and how emotionally and physically traumatic it was for you. Whether it took place in your bathroom, the emergency room, an operating room, or somewhere out in public, you'd recount the anguish you felt when you first sensed the gush of blood or had to go in for a procedure to remove your sweet baby, already in Heaven, from your womb.

No matter if you lost your baby at eight weeks or eight months into your pregnancy or even eight days or eight months after birth, I'd grieve with you for your beloved baby. I firmly believe life begins at conception, and God created each of our babies in His image (Genesis 1:27). Regardless of which medical complications or tragic events led to your baby's death, I believe each of our babies has an eternal soul and spirit that lives forever in Heaven.

Though our stories may differ, I unite with you in our shared heartache. We both lost our hopes and dreams for our babies' lives on earth. We endured the most painful loss a human can experience: the loss of a child. It is quite simply not the way it is supposed to be, even in a broken world where death exists. Parents should not have to bury their children; it's not the natural order.

Whether you lost your baby just a few weeks ago, several years ago, or maybe even decades ago, I want you to know that I am entering back into the waves of fresh grief with you. Though it's been ten years since Bridget went to Heaven, I can keenly remember what the intense grief felt like, especially because I am writing this book in a season of deep sorrow over the tragic and unexpected loss of my beloved dad, who was killed by a drunk driver.

Friend, I am in the trenches with you. I understand that no matter how much time has passed since your baby went to Heaven, you will always mourn your baby. I know there's not a day that goes by that you don't think about them. A decade later, I still think of Bridget daily. I will miss her until I take my last dying breath and open my eyes to see her in Heaven.

I am sure you feel the same. Speaking of how you feel, in the Little Blue Barn, I would ask you how you're doing—I mean, how you're *really* doing. I know you're not "okay" (there's no way to be "fine" in circumstances like these). I'd wait, giving you time to process an honest answer. With me, you don't need to pretend you are doing better than you are. I'm a safe place for your broken heart to land. I'm here to hear the truth of your real emotions.

Nothing you could tell me would scare me away or make me think differently of you. There's no judgment here. I've experienced every imaginable grief emotion there is to feel: sadness, anxiety, anger, bitterness, confusion, doubt, hopelessness, and everything in between.

I know what it feels like to be so sad you wish you could just go to Heaven right now and be with your baby. I've been where you are, and I am with you now. Though physical distance separates us, the Holy Spirit connects our hearts. He's with me, and He's with you. He holds us together. You are not alone in your sadness.

• • • FROM HERE TO HEAVEN • • •

Before we walk this road together, I want you to know where I am leading you. A trip without a planned, final destination would take us somewhere we didn't want or intend to be. Sadly, most people grieve aimlessly, constantly grabbing at the next thing that promises them peace or pleasure. Each desperate attempt to numb their pain only leads them further away from actual healing.

But that's not going to be your story. That's why you're reading this book. You *know* deep down that you need Jesus to get you through this. But where, exactly, is He going to take you? For followers of Jesus, our *final* destination is the New Earth (described in Revelation 21–22), where we will live with Him and our children forever.

This Paradise will be the ultimate pinnacle of perfection, but there's a journey we need to make between *here* and *there*, between *now* and *forever*. It's the one we are on now—living here on this broken earth—as we await the final restoration of all Creation.

We are going to take the journey together, reaching milestones along the way. Remember, Jesus didn't just come to give us eternal life in Heaven but also to provide us with abundant life here on earth. He proclaimed, "I came that they may have life and have it abundantly" (John 10:10 ESV). I believe that His promise of fullness of life includes hope, healing, and joy—even after losing a baby.

Sweet friend, you will not stay in this pit of despair forever. Though I've been in the depths of this pain before, Jesus didn't leave me there. He lifted me out of the muck and mire. After Bridget died, He healed my heart, redeemed my pain, and restored my joy. I trust in His faithfulness and believe He will do it again in my current season of grief. And I am writing this book because I absolutely believe Jesus will do the same for you!

However, I can't promise you the journey will be smooth. Grief is painful, and following Jesus isn't always easy. But I can't let you miss out on the radical redemption and powerful purpose waiting for you as you walk with Jesus through your grief.

So how do you start? You put one foot in front of the other: one minute, one hour, one day at a time. Jesus, the Good Shepherd, will guide you on the straight and narrow road that leads to life (Matthew 7:13–14). He is good, and He's got you, my friend.

• • • THERE IS HOPE • • •

If no one has told you this before, please let me be the first to tell you that I believe God has a wonderful plan for your life, despite this heartbreaking tragedy you have experienced. The death of your baby is not the end of your story.

There is hope! God loves you and your baby more than you can imagine, and He plans to bring you together again. In the meantime, He will heal your heart, and one day, you will use your pain to comfort others. Healing doesn't mean you will forget about your baby or simply move on. No, it's quite the opposite. Healing means you will surrender your suffering to God. You will let Him use your grief for good and for His glory. It means you will remember your baby and honor them by serving others.

Instead of looking back on the pain of your past and the last day you were pregnant or held your baby, you will look forward to the day you will be with them again. So, what do you do as you await that day? That's what we will cover in the latter part of this book. But first, we need to cover some ground on what to do now in the freshness of your grief.

Then we need to build a firm foundation of faith to stand on for the rest of this journey. Because it is one thing to grieve and another to "grieve with hope" (1 Thessalonians 4:13). I'll show you the difference as we go. My prayer for you is that you will trust Jesus to heal your heart as He holds your baby in Heaven.

So, momma, let's meet at the Little Blue Barn and get started. I'm here waiting for you with a hug at the door.[2]

Love,

Ashley

2. You are welcome to visit us at our headquarters in Kansas. I would love to meet (and hug!) you in person at one of our in-person support groups or remembrance events, such as *Wave of Light*, held annually on October 15. Please email us at Info@BridgetsCradles.com before making your travel arrangements.

Prayers to Heaven

Jesus, thank You for bringing us moms together through this book. We wish that our stories were different and that we didn't have to meet under these circumstances. But we need each other, and we need You even more. Will You meet us here? Our hearts are hurting, and we invite You to comfort us. As we journey through Cradled in Hope, *open our hearts to receive Your hope and truth. You are the only One who can heal us. Thank You for dying on the cross and making a way for us to see our babies in Heaven. Because of You, we can grieve with hope. We love You. Amen.*

Truth to Cling To

Psalm 71:12; Psalm 22:5; Psalm 34:17–19; Matthew 11:28; John 6:37; 1 Peter 5:7; Revelation 22:17

Time with Jesus

1. Answer honestly: How are you *really* doing? Reflect on how you're feeling as you begin this journey with Jesus. What are the top five emotions you feel on a day-to-day basis?

2. Is there anything preventing you from *coming as you are*? Identify any roadblocks that prevent you from being vulnerable in this process, and then surrender them to the Lord.

3. Imagine what it would look like if Jesus healed your heart. What evidence would you see? Write five Hope

Statements you'd like to see come to fruition as you read this book. Here are some examples, but feel free to write your own:

- I hope to grow closer to Jesus in my grief.
- I hope to know God's Word better.
- I hope to feel more joy (or feel less sad).
- I hope to find purpose in my pain (or use my grief for good).
- I hope to honor my baby's life.
- I hope to forgive myself and others who have hurt me in my grief.
- I hope to have an eternal perspective (or fix my eyes on Heaven).

We will revisit your Hope Statements at the end of the book, as I am confident the Lord will do a work in and through you by the time we finish.

HEALING STEPS

1. Listen to episodes 1 and 35 of the *Cradled in Hope* podcast to hear me formally welcome you on this journey. The podcast is available on Apple Podcasts, Spotify, and our website at BridgetsCradles.com/Podcast. Our blog features show notes and a full transcript for every episode. We also have bonus episodes called the "Cradled in Hope Book Club" for each chapter of this book.

2. Download the free *Cradled in Hope (CIH) Guided Journal* at AshleyOpliger.com/Journal. The *CIH Guided Journal* will be your companion guide for this book and contains extra hope-filled resources for your journey.

3. Share your baby's story with me at BridgetsCradles.com /ShareYourStory. You can choose whether to keep it private or allow us to publicly share it on our blog. Writing and sharing your baby's story with others can be incredibly healing.

1

Sitting with Jesus

WHEN YOU ARE OVERWHELMED WITH SADNESS

> The LORD is close to the brokenhearted
> and saves those who are crushed in spirit.
>
> Psalm 34:18

I passed out note cards and pens to a group of grieving moms gathered in a circle inside the Little Blue Barn. I instructed everyone to write down words that came to mind when they thought of the word *grief*.

I asked, "What does grief look like in your life? What does it *feel* like?" Pens scribbled away, and one by one, they read their answers out loud:

Pain. Loss. Suffering. Sadness. Crying. Disorienting. Darkness. Disappointment. Unpredictable. Never-ending. Drowning. Heavy. Longing. Lonely. Overwhelming. Roller coaster.

Waves. Deep. Empty. Broken. Heartache. Numbing. Isolating. Anxiety. Depression. Uncontrollable. Sorrow. Shattered. Hollow. Absence. Consuming. Unraveling. Lost. Nightmare. Inescapable. Despair. Agony.

With each word spoken, we nodded in agreement: Yes, this is what grief *feels* like. But what *is* grief? Is it solely a collection of these distressing feelings, or is there more to it than meets the eye—or heart?

On the surface, grief feels like *pain*. But when you peel back its layers, you will uncover its true source: *love*. Grief is a deep sorrow expressing love for someone you cherish who is no longer with you. The words we shared were the *symptoms* of grief, not the *source*. I've heard it stated this way: "Grief is the last act of love we give to our loved one. Where there is deep grief, there is great love."[1]

The day Bridget was born into Heaven was both the best and worst day of my life. Though I was overwhelmed with sadness over her death, the prevailing emotion I felt while holding her was *love*—the unconditional, all-consuming love of a mother.

Holding my sweet girl in her cradle and kissing her tiny lips was one of the best moments of my life. Yet, I was heartbroken holding her lifeless body and seeing death take its toll on her. My love and sorrow for her were so intricately intertwined that I couldn't tell where one emotion started and the other ended. I am sure you've felt this too.

We *grieve* because we first *loved*. Simply put, grief is the price we pay for love, but it is a cost worth counting. The only way to avoid grief is never to love anyone—to walk through life without getting attached to people. Obviously, this is no way to live, especially as parents.

God has given us natural instincts to love, protect, and nurture our children. When we lose a child, grieving is how we love, protect, and nurture their *memory* since we cannot love, protect, and nurture them in the flesh. Our grief affirms the value of our baby's life and validates the magnitude of our loss.

"Grief is just love with no place to go. It's all the love you want to give but cannot."[2] This quote echoes the sentiment that grief is an instinctual response of loving and then losing. Two tiny pink lines appeared, and your heart instantaneously held a lifetime of love for your baby. As God began to knit their sweet body in your womb, you were eternally bonded to your baby as their mother.

But where does your love for them go when they die? How do you love your baby when they're in Heaven and you're still on earth? I understand why some people feel *grief is love with no place to go*, but I would beg to differ. Our love *does* have a place to go.

Your love for your baby is not lost, nor is your baby lost. Your baby is in Heaven, and one day, Jesus will reunite you with them. Because of Him, your love for your baby never has to end. During this time of temporary separation, loving your baby will look different than you had expected or hoped. But there are many fulfilling ways you can express your love for your baby while you wait to hold them in your arms in Heaven.

The grief of a mother is powerful because *love* is powerful. If channeled for good and God's glory, your love for your child holds the tremendous power to change *you* and the *world*. But first, you need to give yourself permission to grieve—even if it has been months or even years since your baby went to Heaven.

I will show you how to find a *physical place* to take your grief, but really the secret is in finding the perfect *Person* to meet you there. If we need to find somewhere for our love to go, we have found our answer in Jesus, who is the ultimate source of love (1 John 4:16).

He created your baby and promises those who believe in Him that they will spend eternity with their babies in Heaven. Jesus also promises to hold you in your grief because He is *Emmanuel*, the God who is *with* us (Matthew 1:23). He has not left you; His presence is always with you.

He is the Creator of your heart and the only One who knows how to put the shattered pieces back together. So, wherever you are in your grief journey, I encourage you to let Jesus sit with you in your sadness. He can relate to your suffering better than anyone else who has walked this earth.

• • • INTO THE FIRE • • •

I love the story of Shadrach, Meshach, and Abednego in the book of Daniel. It's a beautiful illustration of Jesus' presence with us in times of suffering. These brave Jewish men, who lived in Babylon under Nebuchadnezzar II's rule, refused to bow down to the king's golden statue. As a result of their disobedience, they were bound and thrown into a fiery furnace.

While in the fire, a fourth man appeared, whom many believe was the preincarnate[1] Jesus (Daniel 3:25). Nebuchadnezzar was astonished and called the three men out of the fire. Notice Jesus did not appear and rescue them *out* of the fire. Instead, He stood *in* the fire *with* them and protected them from the inferno.

Because *He was there*, the men stayed in the fire, even though they were no longer bound. In the same way, you will not be alone when you walk through the fire of suffering—Jesus will be with you, protecting you as the fire rages around you. The prophet Isaiah declared that when we pass through the waters, He will be with us, and when we walk through the fire, we will not be burned; the flames will not set us ablaze (43:2).

If we accidentally touched an open flame, our survival instincts would kick in and protect us from the *physical* pain. Signals instantly tell us to immediately pull our hand away. Our brains respond similarly to grief and trauma in an attempt to shield us from *emotional* pain—which can be both helpful and harmful.

1. *Preincarnate* refers to the existence of Christ prior to His incarnation as Jesus.

Grieving is a painful experience, and sometimes, our brains want us to avoid feeling the pain in an effort to protect us. However, to heal, we actually need to confront our grief by walking directly *through the fire* with Jesus. Without Him, the flames will inevitably scathe us.

We may try to numb our pain by turning to unhealthy coping mechanisms such as drinking, doing drugs, overeating, overspending, mindless scrolling, being promiscuous, self-harming, or acting out of character. But these coping mechanisms are like putting a Band-Aid on a gaping wound. They simply won't heal the hurt deep inside.

Over time, these behaviors can develop into addictions and veer us away from the life God desires for us. Turning to sin rather than surrendering our pain to Him can result in unwanted repercussions such as bitterness, resentment, anger, depression, anxiety, and shame—stealing our joy and ruining our relationships.

This is why it's so important to grieve *with Him* even when others are pressuring you to move on. Do you have friends or family members who expect you to act like your old self and do the things you used to do? Do you have coworkers or clients who haven't acknowledged your loss and expect you to show up to work and pretend that nothing happened?

Our culture lacks sensitivity and holds unspoken expectations for the grieving, such as *Move on! Be strong. Get over it! Don't talk about it.* These subliminal messages make us push our feelings down and pretend we are okay. We don't want to burden others with our sorrow when we can sense they want us to get back to normal.

People are uncomfortable sitting in others' sadness. They feel awkward when we talk about our babies who have died because they don't know what to say. Often, they will say the wrong things, and sometimes, they won't say anything at all, which hurts even more.

If no one has acknowledged your loss or validated your grief, please know you have every right to be sad over losing your precious baby. No matter how many weeks you carried them, their life is worthy of being grieved, along with all the hopes and dreams you had for them. It's okay to mourn the life, family, and future you had envisioned with your child.

We need to allow ourselves time and space to grieve even when others have moved on and have stopped checking in on us. Even if it feels like no one else cares anymore, it's important to carve out dedicated grieving time in your schedule. Although you may feel left behind and lonely, your private season of grieving is vital to your healing. It's true what they say, "You have to feel to heal." It is worth spending time grieving rather than rushing back into the demands of your regular routine.

I can still remember the sound of the wind chimes on our back deck as I sat in the stillness of our living room. A friend gave us the chimes right after Bridget went to Heaven. They were tuned to my favorite hymn, "Amazing Grace," and I found great comfort in hearing them during my leave from work.

My employer graciously granted me eight weeks off after Bridget's birth, allowing me time to grieve. During those two months, I cried, prayed, and journaled every single day in the solitude of our home after my husband went to work for the day.

The chimes played a heavenly composition as they clanged in the wind, reminding me I wasn't alone. The Lord was with me in my loneliness. I'm grateful I spent that sacred season grieving with Him before returning to work and my daily routine. But not everyone is generously granted time off after they lose a baby.

Maybe your employer expects you to be back at work sooner than you're ready to be, or perhaps you have living children you still need to take care of. Whatever your circumstances, you probably feel the tension between the never-ending demands of life and the grief that weighs heavily on your shoulders. What do you do when people expect you to return to normal, but you're just trying to survive?

• • • SURVIVAL MODE • • •

For starters, it is imperative that you take care of yourself—as best you can, given the circumstances—and allow others to care for you too. It might seem overly simplistic to offer you this advice, but in the days of fresh grief, it's important to focus on two basic life functions: eating and sleeping (both of which are hard to do).

Your appetite is low, and your mind won't stop racing at night. It's hard to fall asleep, stay asleep, or both. You wake up early in the morning only to remember that your baby is still gone, and you must face another day without them. It is an awful feeling.

When Elijah was suffering in the wilderness in 1 Kings 19, he sat under a tree and prayed that he would die. "I have had enough, Lord. Take my life," he cried out in agony (1 Kings 19:4). Elijah slept, and God sent an angel to minister to him by offering him food and drink. Why? Because he needed strength for the journey ahead.

The same is true for you, my sister. I won't sugarcoat the fact that your healing journey is going to be long and hard. You were forced to say good-bye to your baby before you even got to say hello. Losing your precious baby in such a sudden, unexpected way is worthy of the level of grief you are feeling.

But in order to walk this road with Jesus, you will need your physical strength. And you'll need to gain that strength in super simple ways because navigating complex habits is hard when your life has fallen apart. So, may I offer some practical advice for caring for yourself while in this survival stage?

- Take a nap during the day if you didn't sleep well the night before. It's okay, I promise. Go to bed early if you can.

- In the morning, let the light in! Open the blinds on as many windows as you can in your house. This simple act in the morning can have a dramatically positive impact on the rest of your day.
- Fill a large, refillable bottle (preferably glass or stainless steel, 30–40 oz.) with filtered or distilled water in the morning and try to drink it before the afternoon, refilling and finishing it once more before bedtime. Staying hydrated is so important.
- Purchase protein bars and shakes for easy, convenient protein sources. Cheese sticks, beef sticks, protein yogurts, and granola are some of my other go-to options for high-protein snacks.
- Though eating junk food and sweets may be tempting, try to eat as much healthy, whole-food nutrition as possible. When I am sad, I often run to food for comfort. However, I usually eat processed foods high in carbs or sugar that don't make me feel my best. Fueling my body with healthy foods has helped me tremendously in my grief (though it certainly takes more time and energy to eat healthy, so just do the best you can).
- For the time being, accept meals from other people. Say yes to a Meal Train. Allow yourself to get takeout more often than you usually do. Make easy "throw-together" meals, and don't feel guilty about it. The time will come when you're cooking and baking again, but that time is not now. Do what you can, knowing this is a temporary season and that things like cooking will get easier.
- When deep in grief, old healthy habits often go by the wayside (understandably so). Try to simplify them or ask for help (e.g., lay out your vitamins in an easy-to-remember place, have a friend assist you with meal prep, wash fresh fruit for the week).

- Daily chores can feel so overwhelming. Buy paper plates, bowls, and disposable silverware and use them instead of your normal dinnerware for now. This small, temporary investment will drastically reduce the number of dishes you need to clean at the end of the day when your energy is depleted.

- Don't expect to be as productive as you used to be. It's normal to function at a limited capacity when you're grieving. Give yourself grace. Don't judge a day's value based on what you accomplished. Focus instead on what God is doing in your heart and who you are becoming.

- Go on a walk outside. Walking is incredibly healing for your body and brain. Being outside in God's Creation is good for your physical, emotional, mental, and spiritual health. Listen to a podcast, sermon, or worship music as you walk. Call a friend and catch up, or leave someone a long voice message (like I've been known to do). Or leave the earbuds at home and have a "walk and talk" with Jesus, praying to Him as you go. Invite a friend to join you. I love getting my steps in while filling my social and spiritual cups at the same time.

- If walking isn't your thing, what is your favorite form of exercise? I enjoy lifting weights, but maybe you'd prefer swimming, going on a bike ride, or attending a workout or dance class. I am not a health or fitness expert by any means, but I have seen how much my mental and spiritual health improve when I move my body.

- If movement feels too daunting right now, spend some time in nature. Sit on your porch or back deck and watch birds fly from tree to tree. Right after my dad went to Heaven, this was one of the only things that brought me comfort (especially when blue jays stopped by).

- Get a massage or facial. I know it might feel wrong to let your body relax and do something for yourself, but it's good for you occasionally.

Lastly, don't confuse caring for yourself with falling into the trap of the "self-help Gospel." It's not the same thing. If self-care is the focus of your healing and the source of your hope, then that's obviously a major problem. But if Jesus is at the center of your healing and He is the sole source of your hope, then making healthy choices to care for your body is simply being a wise steward of the temple He gave you.

Let Jesus and His angels minister to you in physical ways. Try to get some quality sleep, drink some clean water, eat some healthy food, and relax your body. These simple principles are foundational to your overall wellness in a season of grief. I know from personal experience the chaos that ensues in my mind and body when I neglect taking care of myself.

So, yes, self-care will help you, but Jesus will be the One to heal you. He is with you in the tunnel of darkness we call grief. The clouds will clear soon, and the Son will shine through. You may not see it now, but by faith, I know His light is coming. In the meantime, it's important to spend time in the tunnel, sitting with Jesus in your sadness and grieving the loss of your baby.

• • • How Do I Grieve? • • •

Every Friday after Bridget passed away, I brought fresh flowers in a mason jar to her grave. The jar was special because it was the same one I used to bring flowers to her at the funeral home—the last time I held her before they placed her inside her casket.

During my pregnancy with her, Fridays were the days I turned another week pregnant. On Fridays, I would take my weekly "bump picture" with a sticker on my growing belly displaying the number of weeks she was. Sadly, we only made it to sticker twenty-four. After she passed away, I decided not to toss the remaining stickers. Instead, each Friday, I stuck one on a mason jar filled with flowers and photographed them at her grave, documenting my grief journey up until her due date.

Not only was I missing her, but I was also mourning no longer being pregnant with her. My womb—and heart—felt so empty without her. Those "Flower Fridays," as I called them, were my way of grieving each week that went by without her. This was one of the many ways I grieved in those early weeks. You will find your own ways that are meaningful to you. We each have unique personalities and grieve differently.

There is no perfect formula for grieving. Don't feel pressured to check off the boxes or do things a certain way—something I struggled with early in my journey. I so desperately wanted to honor Bridget's life that I became anxious when I wasn't doing enough or living up to the high standards I had set for myself.

The ideas I am about to share are suggestions to consider, not a checklist to follow. Listen to your heart, let yourself feel your feelings, and process your grief with Jesus in ways that are personal and healing to you.

Crying is a healthy way to pour out your heart's sorrow for your baby. I found that in the midst of my fresh grief, allowing myself at least one really good, heartfelt cry each day was the emotional release I needed. Or maybe you work through your pain best by journaling, praying, or listening to worship music.

Maybe you need to listen to a Christian grief podcast (like the one I host called *Cradled in Hope*) or a sermon from a biblically sound pastor. Going through a Bible study or devotion can also be very therapeutic. Talking to your friends and family about your baby and your grief can be helpful too.

You could look at pictures or ultrasounds of your baby or search for grief quotes and Scripture online. Maybe you cuddle or sleep with a teddy bear you bought for your baby or something that physically touched your baby, such as a blanket or cradle, if you received one.

Or maybe you choose to preserve those precious items in a shadow box in your home. You could also make a scrapbook with photographs from your pregnancy or your baby's birth.

You could plant flowers or a tree in their memory. Or plan a memorial service with a balloon, bubble, or butterfly release. Many bereaved moms enjoy wearing memorial jewelry, such as a birthstone necklace with their baby's name or initials.

For some moms, visiting their baby's grave and decorating around their headstone is a form of grieving. For others, holding onto their baby's urn and spending time close to their baby's ashes brings them comfort. For those who are apart from their baby's remains, it can be helpful to have a memorial space in your home or garden to visit.

Because sometimes we need a physical place to take our grief. We seem to have an innate desire to *go somewhere* when we feel sad. We need a place where we can fall apart without the expectation to be "on" or put together. Maybe you're like me and need a private place to grieve your feelings out loud. For me, this sometimes looks like curling up on my closet floor or sitting hunched over on my bed and sobbing until my tears soak a tissue. But other times, even my own home doesn't bring the solace I need.

Sometimes, I drive to Bridget's grave and whisper prayers for Jesus to pass along to her as I reposition the rocks around her headstone—the ones we painted as a family on her last Heavenly birthday. But mostly, my healing home is the Little Blue Barn, where I am typing these words to you. I can't count how many times I have met God here and how much healing He has done in my heart within these walls.

What about you? Do you have a place where you can be vulnerable, cry, and feel spiritually close to God? If you do, I would suggest you spend more time there. If you don't have a place yet, I hope you will find one. Whether it's your bedroom, baby's cemetery, church pew, support group chair, or Christian counselor's couch, I want you to meet Jesus there.

• • • CRADLED IN HIS ARMS • • •

I collapsed on the floor of Bridget's empty nursery. All my strength was gone, and I crumbled under the weight of my grief. I didn't know where to go or what to do with the sadness threatening to suffocate me. I curled my weary body into the fetal position and unleashed my soul's anguish.

Salty tears ran hot down my cheeks, dropping onto the carpet beneath me, one after the other. I let my heart bear its sorrows on the floor in her should-have-been nursery. As dark as my mental and emotional state had become, I knew I needed to feel my feelings—real and raw—in order to move forward.

Many times, in those early days of grief, I would think to myself, "I don't want to let myself *go there*. I'm too scared to let myself *really* feel it. What if I don't come out of it? What if it becomes too hopeless, and I become suicidal?" So instead of going *there*, I would keep myself busy and distracted for fear of how quickly I'd spiral or how sad I would feel.

I put guardrails around my grief to insulate myself from the true intensity of my emotions. But grief has a way of catching up to you, even when you don't want it to. Friend, I know you want the agonizing pain to go away. You're desperate for your heart to stop hurting so badly. You want to feel like you can breathe again, smile again, even laugh again—without grief threatening to steal every fleeting moment of joy you temporarily encounter.

It can be tempting to bury the pain deep within your soul. But if you delay your grieving, you will only delay your healing. Pain demands to be *felt*. Suppressing your emotions now will only make them resurface later. Real healing comes only *after* real grieving.

Remember the analogy I used when I compared coping mechanisms to a Band-Aid? What do we need instead? It's not a bigger bandage. We need Jesus to heal the wound from the inside out. In biblical times, the Hebrews used salt—a natural antiseptic from the region near the Dead Sea—to disinfect wounds so they could properly heal. However, pouring salt on a wound doesn't feel very good; in fact, it stings and can be quite painful.

In today's usage, the idiom "pouring salt on the wound" has a negative connotation: making a bad situation even worse. And it might feel like grieving God's way is making a sad situation even worse. It doesn't *feel good* to grieve without numbing agents. But, friend, I can promise you that Jesus' salt is what you need to heal. He needs to clean the wound out fully so it can heal properly.

But, oh, this process is painful. It requires opening up your heart and surrendering your sorrows to Him. The Bible contains numerous examples of God's most faithful followers mourning deeply and crying out to Him in prayer, a practice called *lamenting* (see Lamentations, the Psalms, and the book of Job). The Hebrew words for lament mean "to wail" or "cry out."[3]

To lament, you set aside time to be fully present with God in your grief. Then you let the tears flow and tell Him how much you love and miss your baby. Express to Him how badly you are hurting. Your emotions, fears, and doubts won't scare Him away. He can handle your honest feelings and tough questions.

He is your Heavenly Daddy, a good Father who loves you and longs to comfort you. Growing up, my earthly dad modeled what this kind of love was like. He would hug me and my siblings and say, "Can you feel my love arrows?" We would squeeze him back and tell him our hearts received his love.

I now use this endearing term with my two sons, both when giving them hugs and when we're apart by saying, "I'm sending you my love arrows." We also refer to our hearts as love tanks and say things like, "Let's snuggle and fill each other's love tanks" or "My love tank is empty; I need some love."

There's a quote I stumbled upon while searching quotes on Pinterest in the days after Bridget's death that spoke directly to my heart: "Jesus, I wanted to sit my baby on my lap and tell them about You. As I can't do that now, will You sit them on Your knee and tell them about me?"⁴ The imagery of Jesus holding Bridget would become a great comfort to me in my grief.

We would later choose to have Psalm 139:14—"I praise You because I am fearfully and wonderfully made"—along with an image of Jesus holding a baby engraved on her headstone. Each time I visit her grave and see her headstone, I am reminded that He is holding her.

Though her body is buried there, *she* is not in her grave. Bridget is *in* Jesus' physical presence in Heaven, and as a follower of Jesus, His Holy Spirit is *in* me. We are *both* in His presence, meaning Heaven is much closer than we think! Jesus directly connects us to our babies through His Spirit.

He is the conduit that carries my love arrows to Bridget. But unlike on earth, where our love tanks can sometimes feel empty, hers is always full. She is held by the Source of love, Jesus. So, friend, will you imagine Him cradling you in His loving arms as He cradles your baby in Heaven? Can you picture Him passing your love arrows to your baby?

Hear Him say to you, "Sweet daughter of Mine, I know you're hurting, and I'm hurting with you. I'm here with you in your pain, and I will one day wipe away all your tears. I know you miss your baby so much. I am holding them now and will take good care of them until you arrive. I'm telling them about you—wonderful stories about their amazing momma. Don't you worry, I'm giving them all My love and passing on your love too. I will reunite you with them soon. Until then, I'm never going to leave your side. I love you, My daughter. Will you sit with Me and let Me hold you for a while?"

PRAYERS TO HEAVEN

Jesus, You are so loving and kind. You are close to our broken hearts, and You desire to sit with us in our sadness. Help us grieve our precious babies and express our love for them during this time of temporary separation. With the world pressuring us to move on and grieve faster, help us to slow down and truly lament. Let us feel Your presence as we bring our pain to You. Heal our hearts in the way that only You can. Cradle us in Your arms as You cradle our babies in Heaven. We love You, Amen.

TRUTH TO CLING TO

Psalm 6:6; Psalm 23:3; Isaiah 40:28–29; Jeremiah 31:15; Lamentations 3:19–33; Matthew 5:4; Luke 10:38–42

TIME WITH JESUS

1. What does grief look like in your life? What does it feel like? Write down a list of words that come to mind when you think of the word *grief*.
2. Have you been avoiding your grief or turning to negative coping mechanisms? Reflect on any tendency you have to numb your pain instead of surrendering it to God.
3. As the Lord leads, and as much as you are able to, try to slow down. Can you say no to something or delegate it to someone else for a while? Can you remove or reschedule an obligation on your calendar to free up some extra time? List ways you can give yourself time to grieve.

HEALING STEPS

1. Grief is a symptom of love. Spend time doing something to express your love for your baby. Pick an idea mentioned in this chapter or from the Bridget's Cradles e-book *Memorial Ideas for a Baby in Heaven* that comes as a resource when you download the free *CIH Guided Journal* from my website, AshleyOpliger.com/Journal.

2. Friend, when was the last time you allowed yourself to cry? I'm talking about a let-your-walls-down, look-at-yourself-in-the-mirror, ugly-sob kind of cry. It may sound strange to schedule a cry, but giving yourself time to lament is important.

3. Take your grief *somewhere*. If you already have a place, spend time there sitting with Jesus in your sadness. If you don't have one, try to find one, whether it's a comfy corner of your home or a peaceful place in nature.

2

Broken and Bleeding

WHEN YOU FEEL ABANDONED BY GOD

How long, LORD? Will you forget me forever?
How long will you hide your face from me?
How long must I wrestle with my thoughts
and day after day have sorrow in my heart?

Psalm 13:1–2

Trigger Warning:[1] medical trauma

The week before Bridget was born, my daily bleeding from a previously diagnosed subchorionic hemorrhage began to increase. After filling several pads in an hour, I went to the hospital. They admitted me to the antepartum floor, and shortly after, I started passing large blood clots, some the size of a golf ball.

---

1. To be as sensitive as possible to my readers, I've included Trigger Warnings at the start of chapters that feature content or stories that might be difficult to read, depending on one's past experiences or current struggles.

My cervix was beginning to dilate at twenty-three weeks gestation, and I feared this was going to be the end of my pregnancy—and even worse, the end of Bridget's life. I lay terrified in the hospital bed as they wrapped the fetal monitor straps around my small but growing belly.

I stared intently at the monitor screen, waiting and hoping to hear the sound of her beating heart. Moments later, I could see the lines tracing her heartbeat rhythm—tiny squiggles up and down moving in unison with the *thump thump thump* that now filled the room.

Over the next few hours, I alternated between two locations: lying in bed in agonizing pain and then into the bathroom where nurses transported me to pass another clot into the toilet. Each time, the pressure sensation made me fear I would deliver Bridget there. The nurses, with their gloved hands, combed through the blood in the toilet and assured me she had not been born.

It was traumatic, and I wondered, *Is this how it all ends?* Little did I know that her birth would occur one week later, in a different room at the same hospital. But this night, I vividly remember lying in the hospital bed, broken and bleeding. I stared at the tiled ceiling above me in a daze as I fixated on the sound of Bridget's heartbeat. As I did, I started to see visions of Jesus' crucifixion on the ceiling, almost as though a projector was casting images above me.

I didn't see Jesus' face specifically, but I saw His figure on the cross. The vision was lifelike, as if I were standing at a distance at Calvary, witnessing His execution. I could see flesh ripped from His skin. He was exhausted and weak. His physical pain was not only visible but palpable—unbearable, unimaginable.

Hot tears ran down the sides of my face, absorbing into the sterile hospital pillow beneath me. I didn't wipe them as they fell. I just lay frozen—watching in equal parts horror and reverence—at what my Savior endured for me. Being in my own physical agony, I connected with His suffering in a way I hadn't before.

No, my pain wasn't the same, and I wasn't trying to compare my suffering to His. But the experience of being in pain myself as I envisioned His crucifixion allowed me to witness His humanness in a way I hadn't before. As I lay bleeding, I saw His bloody body hanging on the cross crying out, "*Eli, Eli, lema sabachthani?*" which means "My God, my God, why have you forsaken me?" (Matthew 27:46). In His despair, Jesus questioned whether His Father had abandoned Him. Have you ever felt this way? I know I have, especially during my pregnancy with Bridget. I felt forsaken during those eleven weeks of bleeding. I questioned whether she would survive the complications in my womb. Would God answer my prayers and save her?

I was a good mother who *wanted* my baby. We had conceived Bridget in marriage and were committed to raising her to follow Jesus. Why would God allow this to happen to good parents who wanted nothing more than to raise their children to love Him?

This brought me back to the age-old theological question: *Why do bad things happen to good people?* Though countless people have written books and articles on this topic, R.C. Sproul Jr. had the most profound response I've heard, "That only happened once, and He volunteered."[1]

His answer highlights the important truth that we are not good people—not you, me, or anyone else on this earth. Paul proclaimed, "All have sinned and fall short of the glory of God" (Romans 3:23 ESV). No one is righteous, not even one (Romans 3:10).

We live in a broken world devoid of justice. Good things happen to "good" and "bad" people, and bad things happen to "good" and "bad" people. God "makes his sun rise on the evil and on the good, and sends rain on the just and on the unjust" (Matthew 5:45 ESV). In other words, the ill effects of sin affect *everyone* on earth.

God does not simply dole out punishment to those who sin and blessings upon those who are righteous. Pregnancy loss, for example, affects women of all nationalities, ages, races, and faith backgrounds. It happens to mothers who love and follow Jesus and those who don't.

The issues that cause babies to die in the womb are a result of the Fall, just like cancer and other diseases. God did not handpick us for this awful assignment *because of our specific sins*. Our babies died *because of sin*—that is, the *original sin* that brought death into the world. John chapter 9 clarifies this critical distinction.

Jesus and His disciples encounter a man who has been blind since birth. His disciples ask Him who sinned—the man or his parents—to cause the man to be born blind. Jesus responded that neither the man nor his parents sinned. Instead, He said, "This happened so that the works of God might be displayed in his life" (v. 3).

The same is true of miscarriage and stillbirth. Your baby's death did not happen as a result of your sin or your baby's— given that they hadn't even had a chance to sin. It happened because, in our broken world, some babies sadly die before they are born. Though I don't understand it, and I wish it weren't so, God can display a beautiful work through their life and yours. What the enemy meant for evil, God can use for good (see Genesis 50:20).

So, while it's true that the death of our babies is not good, it's also true that God can bring good from it. The two are not mutually exclusive. Jesus, our Redeemer, specializes in turning ashes into beauty (see Isaiah 61:3). But right now, in the messy middle of grief, it's hard to see that with tear-stained vision. You feel like a shell of a person and can't imagine anything good coming from this.

Oh, friend, I've been there. I'm here again right now. It feels like your whole life has been flipped upside down, and you feel disoriented and unmoored. For even the strongest of believers, it can be a confusing and faith-shaking time. Maybe you're like me, and the death of your baby caused you to experience a *crisis of faith*—a moment that forced you to decide what you *really* believe about God, Jesus, and Heaven.

⬩ ⬩ ⬩ IS MY FAITH REAL? ⬩ ⬩ ⬩

Whether you believed in God before the loss of your baby or not, this unexpected tragedy may have challenged you to ponder what you think about life after death. Consequently, it puts you in a position to determine what you believe about Jesus, the only person in history who defeated death and left behind an empty tomb.

What does His life have to do with yours? This is a good question to ask because the answer matters now more than ever. In *A Grief Observed*, C. S. Lewis asserts, "You never know how much you really believe anything until its truth or falsehood becomes a matter of life and death to you."[2]

For some moms, experiencing a traumatic event like the loss of a child might bring them closer to God and strengthen their faith. However, for others, it might cause them to question their beliefs and consider turning away from Him. Sadly, I've seen women deconstruct their faith after losing a baby, unable to reconcile their belief in a good God who would allow such a tragedy to happen to them.

Whether you are strong in your faith or struggling, I can empathize. As someone who has loved Jesus my whole life, I still experienced the tension of questioning whether what I believed was really true. Most of us do at some point, even if our parents raised us in the faith.

When we reach adolescence or adulthood, our trials end up putting our faith to the test, giving us the opportunity to make our faith our own. Undoubtedly, the death of a baby brings up some hard questions, such as: *What do I believe about Heaven and God? Do I believe what the Bible says? Is my faith real?*

Friend, I want to permit you to explore these questions. I promise it's better to wrestle with God through these deep theological questions than it is to abandon your faith. Throughout this book, I hope to address some of the areas where you might have doubts. As you search for answers, it's not unusual to find that your heart disagrees with your head.

What do I mean by that? Maybe you're trying to reconcile what you *know* to be true about God with how you *feel* about Him. You *know* God is real, but you can't *feel* His presence. You *believe* He is good, but He doesn't *feel* good right now. Your head knowledge about God isn't lining up with how your heart feels about Him.

I completely get it. It's normal to feel this way, but let me explain why this so easily happens. The loss of a loved one elicits far more than just an intellectual response; it warrants an emotional response. Death causes a grief so deep that it impacts your entire heart, mind, and soul.

But this becomes problematic when we start to "think" with our feelings rather than with the wisdom and knowledge of God. Your heart holds tremendous power because your feelings about God influence your thoughts about Him. Typically, it plays out like this:

Circumstances ⟶ Feelings ⟶ Thoughts ⟶ Perception of God

Your circumstances influence how you feel, which influences how you think, which changes your perception of God.

However, this model has two massive problems: (1) Our circumstances shouldn't determine our view of God, and (2) we shouldn't trust our hearts. In the words of Jeremiah, "The heart is deceitful above all things" (Jeremiah 17:9). So we need to reverse the flow to this:

Truth of God ⟶ Thoughts ⟶ Feelings ⟶
Perception of Circumstances

God's Word has the power to transform your thoughts, which shape your emotions and, ultimately, shift how you perceive your circumstances. We want our faith to inform our feelings, not the other way around. When our feelings inform our "truth," we develop a skewed perception of who God is.

What is truth, anyway? We live in a generation that primarily subscribes to *postmodern relativism*, the idea that there's no absolute truth and everyone can have their own "truth." Paul warned us there would come a time when people would follow what their "itching ears" wanted to hear and not listen to sound doctrine (2 Timothy 4:3). He prophesied about the times we live in now, saying, "They will turn their ears away from the truth and turn aside to myths" (v. 4).

The "live your truth" and "you do you" mentality is pervasive in our current culture. But if *your* truth and *my* truth differ or oppose each other, it can't be possible that both are true. Obviously, not everyone's subjective truth can be true simultaneously. If it were, there would be no truth whatsoever.

There has to be one objective, absolute Truth, which cannot be attached to the faulty feelings of sinful humans. The created (humans) do not have the authority to *establish* truth. Only the Creator (God) has that authority, but we can *subscribe* to it.

In other words, our truth is only true if it aligns with His Truth. The Bible is the standard and source of Truth. Paul told us *all* Scripture is God-breathed and profitable for teaching, reproof, correction, and training in righteousness (2 Timothy 3:16–17 ESV). We cannot take scissors to God's Word and cut out the parts we don't like. It's all or nothing—believe it all or leave it all.

This can be difficult after experiencing the soul-shattering loss of a baby. Parts of His Word may not make sense to us or *feel* good. When this happens, we have a tendency to either disregard it as false or misconstrue it to make us feel better. This is a dangerous slippery slope into bad theology that will negatively impact our relationship with God. Here's how it happens:

Misinterpret God's Word

↓

Misunderstand God's Character

↓

Mistrust God

When we misinterpret God's Word, we can unknowingly believe in a false gospel, which is any message that "excludes, alters, or replaces any of the key components of the Gospel as outlined in Scripture."[3] One of the most common false gospels is the *prosperity gospel*—the teaching that if we follow God and do the right things, we will have health, wealth, and happiness. If we are a "good person" and love Jesus, He will bless us and protect us from all harm.

Sadly, this discrepancy in expectations is why the death of a baby catapults many mothers into feeling deep disappointment and mistrust in Him. Surely a good God wouldn't allow this to happen to good mothers like us, so we conclude that one or more of the following must be true:

- God must not be good.
- He must be punishing me for something I've done.
- I must not be a good person.
- He must not love me.

Do you see how destructive this line of thinking is? If we believe God will protect us from hardship, we are in for a rude awakening when we face trials of many kinds. Unfortunately, being a Christian doesn't give us immunity against the problems of this world.

On the contrary, Jesus told us that following Him would be costly and difficult (Luke 9:23–27, 57–62; 14:25–33). The prosperity gospel, while clearly not biblical, is deeply ingrained in many of our belief systems. I didn't realize I had fallen victim to it until I reflected on the inner dialogue I had with God during my days on bed rest with Bridget:

Why, God? Why are You allowing this? I am a good Christian. I follow You. How could You let this happen to me? How dare You, God!

Can you spot the core beliefs hiding beneath the surface of my questions?

- I don't deserve this.
- Because I love You, You should protect me from pain.
- If I follow You, I expect You to bless me.

These erroneous beliefs wreaked havoc on my relationship with God and made me feel abandoned by Him. If you've personally experienced this and want to dig deeper into how we adopt these faulty beliefs, please see appendix 1, "Errors in Our Theology," on page 251. In it, I explore the importance of proper biblical interpretation and how it impacts our view of God.

• • • SCRIPTURE BALM • • •

So how do you combat the perception of feeling abandoned by God? The best answer I can muster may seem overly simplistic, but I promise it's not trite advice: Read your Bible to remind yourself who He is.

He is a personal and present God who longs to be—and *is*—near to your broken heart. He is trustworthy through every circumstance, even this one. In chapter 6, we will explore some of God's attributes, but I want you to know that His Word is the first place you should turn when you're feeling forsaken.

Scripture is a healing balm for your hurting heart. Applying the ointment of God's Word generously and frequently will bring healing day after day. It is the sustenance you need in your sadness—the daily bread you will feed on to help you through your grief (see Matthew 6:11).

But right now, it may be hard to crack open your Bible when the book itself feels heavy. I know it took an act of strength for you to even pick up *this* book right now. The throes of grief make it hard to do even the simplest of tasks. I can imagine you are having trouble sleeping; you are tossing and turning, and waking intermittently throughout the night—each time being reminded that the nightmare you are living is a reality you can't wake up from: Your baby is gone.

You awake in the morning exhausted and sick to your stomach. The nights and mornings seem to be the hardest parts of the day. You barely have the strength to get out of bed. It feels like a brick is on your chest, threatening to suffocate you. You pace around your house, not knowing what to do with yourself or how to make the deep pain in your heart subside. You try to go through the motions and get a few things done, but being productive—like you used to be—feels impossible.

If this is you, friend, I am so sorry. Grief is incredibly lonely, isolating, and all-consuming. It feels like all the joy has been sucked from your life, never to return to you again. You feel like you are merely surviving, not *living*, mustering everything inside of you to just make it through another day. Yet you dread the sun going down because it means you must endure another painful night.

You *know* the answer is Jesus, but why doesn't "grieving with hope" *feel* better? Shouldn't the hope of Heaven significantly reduce your pain? Shouldn't Jesus' presence bring automatic peace? Why does it hurt so badly even when you believe your baby is in Heaven and you know you'll see him or her again one day?

I have wondered all these things too. You just want the hope you have to *feel* real. But what I've come to realize is that grief is grief, loss is loss, pain is pain—even when you believe in Jesus. These feelings demand to be felt one way or another. The tunnel of grief is going to be dark, regardless of your faith in Him.

However, there are two differences in the tunnel of grief for believers: (1) Jesus promises to be *with* you in the tunnel's darkness, and (2) Jesus promises there will be light at the *end* of the tunnel. This is what it means to grieve with hope.

Yes, the grief is still there, but we are not alone in it. And the best part is that it will not last forever. For Christians, there is an expiration date on our suffering. Though I don't know the exact day, I know with certainty that all mourning, crying, and pain will one day cease (Revelation 21:4).

So, while you're in the thick of it, may I suggest some simple ways to apply Scripture balm to your hurting heart? I recommend listening to the heart cries of the Psalms, which feel so relatable in times of sorrow. Most Bible apps have a play button you can click to hear the audio version if you'd rather listen than read.

I also had a sweet friend send me voice messages of her reading Scripture to me. When I didn't have it in me to open up my Bible, hearing the truth of God's Word spoken over me was such a blessing and balm for my soul. You could also print or purchase Bible verse cards and display them around your home.

Friend, if you feel abandoned by God, you are not alone. I have felt it, as did David when he penned Psalm 13 (this chapter's opening verse). Even Jesus, the Son of God, felt abandoned by His Father when He cried out, "My God, my God, why have you forsaken me?" (Matthew 27:46). Jesus, in His human agony, uttered those words while He hung broken[2] and bleeding on the cross.

At the same time, His Father endured His own suffering as He watched evil men brutally crucify His innocent Son to atone for the sins of the world. This was God's grand purpose for His

2. *Broken* here refers to His broken skin (from being whipped and the crown of thorns on His head). Scripture is clear that His bones were not broken during His crucifixion (John 19:36; Psalm 34:20).

Son's suffering: to save the world through Him (John 3:17)—a redemptive plan He had in place from before time began (John 1:1).

Seven hundred years before Jesus' birth, the prophet Isaiah predicted that the Savior would be a "man of sorrows"—pierced for our transgressions, yet by His wounds, we would be healed (Isaiah 53:1–6 ESV). Jesus took on the punishment we deserved. Our sins nailed Him on the cross to satisfy God's wrath.

As Paul wrote, "God made him who had no sin to be sin for us, so that in him we might become the righteousness of God" (2 Corinthians 5:21). Friend, can you see your suffering Savior dying for you? Though the cross was the object of His torture, it was a display of His magnificent love for you. My sister in Christ, you are not forsaken: You are so dearly loved. The holes in His hands are your proof.

PRAYERS TO HEAVEN

Jesus, in the depths of our despair, we cry out, "Where are You?" We feel abandoned and question whether our faith is real. We need You to draw near to us and keep us in Your Word. We don't want our circumstances to skew our perception of Your character. We want Your Truth to inform our feelings, not the other way around. Help us remember who You are, a good Father who will never leave or forsake us. Remind us of Your great love for us, which Jesus demonstrated on the cross. Amen.

TRUTH TO CLING TO

Deuteronomy 31:8; Psalm 9:10; Psalm 37:28; John 8:32; John 17:17; Romans 5:8; 1 John 4:6–10

Time with Jesus

1. Do you feel abandoned by God? Do you struggle with discrepancies between what your heart feels and what your head knows to be true? Look at the two diagrams on page 58—which flow direction do you most resonate with? Why do you think that is?

2. Does it help to know that your baby's death is not a result of your sin, but of the original sin (that is, the brokenness of the world)? Review the section on page 55 surrounding the question, "Why do bad things happen to good people?" What did you learn? How do you see things differently in light of the Scripture shared?

3. Reflect on your own tunnel of grief. How does the knowledge that Jesus is with you in your tunnel and that there will be light at the end of it change your view of the darkness you are currently experiencing?

Healing Steps

1. Listen to the hymn "Turn Your Eyes Upon Jesus." Reflect on the lyrics, particularly "look full in His wonderful face"[4] and "His Word shall not fail you."[5]

2. Start a Bible reading plan. Whether you go through the Bible in a year or start with the Psalms, Gospels, or New Testament, commit to reading God's Word daily. Personally, I like chronological reading plans.

3. If you're interested in exploring some deeper theology related to the content of this chapter and learning about hermeneutics (how to study the Bible), see appendix 1, "Errors in Our Theology," on page 251.

3

The Gospel Changes Everything

WHEN YOU ARE DESPERATE FOR HOPE

If you declare with your mouth, "Jesus is Lord," and believe in your heart that God raised him from the dead, you will be saved. For it is with your heart that you believe and are justified, and it is with your mouth that you profess your faith and are saved.

Romans 10:9–10

Bridget Faith Opliger was born on October 22, 2014, at 10:27 a.m., weighing 13 ounces and measuring 10.5 inches long. The nurse handed her to us bundled in a traditional hospital receiving blanket.

It was the classic white cotton hospital blanket with tiny pink, blue, and white alternating stripes in the middle, outlined by bolder blue lines. However, the blanket was too large and bulky to hold a baby born in the second trimester. Bridget was so small that it was hard to see her or feel her weight.

When I saw Bridget's tiny frame nestled inside the blanket, I knew I was gazing upon God's most precious creation. I could hardly believe what I was seeing. How did God form such perfection in my bleeding womb? She was fearfully and wonderfully made—every feature so tiny but perfect. Her fingers, long like mine, had the tiniest fingernails. She had a cute button nose with peach fuzz above her little lips.

As we held Bridget in the bulky hospital blanket, my mom reached into her bag and pulled out a beautifully knit mint green cradle. She showed it to us and told us the story of how God had led her to knit it together the week prior, after my last hospital scare. During that visit, the neonatal intensive care unit (NICU) doctors warned us Bridget would likely be born soon due to my heavy bleeding and dilation.

They also diagnosed Bridget with intrauterine growth restriction (IUGR) because her estimated weight was below the fifth percentile. This meant that if she were born early, her veins would be too small for the IVs and medical equipment to save her. Given the poor prognosis, my mom wanted to be a good grandmother and decided to knit a blanket for her granddaughter.

Anticipating Bridget might be born early and very small, my mom realized that a regular-sized blanket wouldn't properly hold her in a dignified way. So she started knitting a small blanket with soft mint green yarn—the same color as my childhood blanket and nursery walls.

As she knit, she wondered how she would swaddle such a tiny baby in a small blanket. That's when God gave her the idea to knit the sides up and turn the blanket into a cradle. Surprisingly, it had never been done before, but God planted the seed of an idea, knowing the eventual fruit that would come from it. That day, the very first "Bridget's cradle" was made in my childhood home in Andover, Kansas.

My mom carefully sewed delicate white lace around the edges of the cradle and added a silver cross charm at the head and a footprint charm at the foot. She didn't tell me she had made the cradle but packed it in the emergency hospital bag she had been preparing in case we needed to go quickly. My mom prayed that Bridget would be born full term and healthy so we wouldn't need to use the little cradle she had made.

However, a week later, we carefully placed Bridget's body in her perfectly sized cradle, wrapped and held in complete love. The cradle was knit together so wonderfully, mirroring how God knit her inside my womb. Even though we knew her soul was in Heaven, holding her body in such a sacred space gave us peace as we loved on her for twenty-four hours.

The cradle changed everything for us. It allowed us to cherish every moment, hold her in front of us, gaze at her face, and bring her to our lips. We could pass her to both Matt's and my immediate family members who came to meet and hold her as she lay snugly in her cradle.

I also had skin-to-skin time with her and delicately caressed her back as her lifeless body rose and fell on my chest—making me realize we were two bodies but only one breath. These sad but sacred moments would be our only mother-daughter moments on this earth, and I did everything I could to savor them.

The following morning, the clock ticked that our time with her was up. Death is ruthless and doesn't allow for more time together when bodies change so quickly without breath in them. Bridget looked so different twenty-four hours later. Her skin was cold and red. A large, purple bruise filled her abdomen. Blood slowly seeped from her nose. The coldness of death reared its ugly head, and seeing her this way broke my heart all over again.

But nothing could have been worse than what happened next. There are no earthly words to describe the pain of saying goodbye to your baby as you hand them over to a funeral home or the hospital's morgue. The anguish of being forced to physically separate from your flesh and blood—your precious child—is something no mother should ever have to endure.

Agony. Despair. Misery. Heartbreak. Torment. Suffering. None of these words is intense enough to describe this feeling. I wept with sobs so deep I could hardly breathe. In all of my life, I can't remember another time I've cried like this. Wailing. Moaning. Hyperventilating. Keening.

From the depths of my soul, my grief was escaping. My body didn't know how to contain it. My heart felt like it shattered into a million pieces and physically left my body, never to come back to me whole again. I wondered if I would die right then and there. Or maybe I just wanted to die to escape the pain I was in—then I could go and be with Bridget in Heaven.

With her lying softly in her cradle, I carefully handed her over and watched as she was carried out of the room. Panicked thoughts immediately raced through my grief-stricken mind: *What now? How will I survive this? How am I supposed to keep on living without her?*

• • • THE BAD NEWS • • •

There's something that feels so final when the bleeding of your miscarriage stops, or the nurse walks away with your baby for the last time. The finality sinks in when fresh dirt is shoveled on top of your baby's casket, or you are handed a small urn with your baby's ashes.

What hurts the most is the physical separation that death has now caused between you and your baby. They were once nestled inside your belly or held safely in your arms, and now you are no longer together. The separation is suffocating.

I have some bad news and good news to share with you. Let's start with the bad news, but I promise the good news is really, really good news—in fact, it's the solution to the bad news. So hold on to hope as you read this section. The bad news is that there's nothing you can do to bring your baby back or to be with them again *right now*.

As much as we wish we had the power to rewind time or reverse the curse of death, we do not. There's nothing *we* can do to fix what death has stolen from us. The sting of death is separation, and *we* don't have the ability to reverse it. I am sure every mom reading this wishes she could have done something differently to prevent the loss of her baby from happening.

I felt that way with Bridget, and I am currently battling those feelings over the recent unexpected loss of my father. When tragedy strikes, we feel completely helpless. We quickly realize we're not God and were never in control to begin with. When things were going well in life, we simply had a false sense of confidence in our own control.

We don't have the power to see into the future, nor can we travel back in time to change the past. It is truly humbling to recognize how very little control we have over anything in our lives, including the lives of our children and other loved ones.

And sadly, this means we cannot control the timing or manner in which our children and loved ones die. This is part of the bad news. I know this can feel *incredibly* unsettling. All we want is to protect those we love from harm's way. However, most circumstances fall outside our ability to control them.

For example, I wish there was something I could have done to prevent my dad from being killed by a drunk driver. I have obsessively ruminated over what I could have possibly done to protect him, wishing I could have changed the timeline of that night so that he wouldn't have been in the path of such a reckless and negligent driver.

But there was no way I could have known that was going to happen to him because I'm not God. When my mind keeps spinning round and round, desperately trying to fix it in my own humanity, I ultimately have to rest my head on the pillow of

God's sovereignty.[1] Likewise, sweet momma, there was no way you could have known this would happen to your baby.

You could not control it. You were not responsible for it. You cannot fix the fact that death has separated you from the precious baby you so desperately wanted and so deeply loved. But where did the separation come from, and will it last forever?

Let's start with the first question. We can trace the root of separation back to the Garden of Eden when Eve's teeth bit into the forbidden fruit. She chose to believe the serpent, who told her that she would become like God if she ate of the Tree of the Knowledge of Good and Evil (Genesis 3:5).

When she took the bite, sin entered the world, and with it, death. God then clothed Adam and Eve with the skin of the first animal sacrifice (Genesis 3:21), the first mention of death in the Bible. Later, in the New Testament, Paul confirmed that death is the consequence of sin (Romans 6:23).

Because God is righteous and holy, He cannot tolerate sin. His "eyes are too pure to look on evil" (Habakkuk 1:13). Sin cannot be in His presence; therefore, sin separates us from Him. Because He is just, He also must judge and punish sin. This is really bad news for us because we are sinners, just like Adam and Eve.

The consequence of sin is eternal separation from Him in a physical place called Hell. Matthew described it as a place of outer darkness where "there will be weeping and gnashing of teeth" (25:30). Mark said it is where "the fire never goes out" (Mark 9:43). Hell is truly horrifying, but because of Jesus' sacrifice and free gift of salvation, sinners don't have to go there.

• • • THE GOOD NEWS • • •

So this is the really good news: *the* Good News of the Gospel! In God's infinite love and mercy, He did not leave us to be eternally separated from Him. He sent His Son, Jesus Christ, to die on the cross for our sins and miraculously rise again! He overcame the grave and put an end to death forever.

In His triumph over death, He offered us a way out of the pits of Hell. He declared, "I am the Living One; I was dead, and now look, I am alive forever and ever! And I hold the keys of death and Hades" (Revelation 1:18). When we place our faith in Him, His blood covers our sins. We need not fear Hell because we are promised eternal life in Heaven with Him.

This is the Gospel, God's sacrificial plan to restore a relationship with Him. It can be traced throughout the Bible's overarching story, also known as the metanarrative of Scripture. In appendix 2, The Simple Gospel, I offer a chart explaining the Gospel in four parts: *Creation, Fall, Redemption,* and *Restoration.*

In summary, God sent Jesus to save us from our sins because we couldn't save ourselves or measure up to God's holy standards. Jesus is God's redemption plan to restore a broken creation and humanity to Himself. As it was in the beginning, it will be in the end. Adam and Eve were originally *with* God *in* the Garden of Eden: "Then the man and his wife heard the sound of *the* LORD *God as He was walking in the garden*" (Genesis 3:8, emphasis added).

And God's final plan is to be with His people again! In Revelation 21:3, John describes the New Earth and reiterates three times in one sentence that God will dwell with His people: "God's dwelling place is now among the people, and he will dwell with them. They will be his people, and God himself will be with them and be their God."

He was in the Garden with Adam and Eve at the beginning (when mankind first rejected Him), and He will be with His people in the restored Garden at the end. In between these two gardens, Jesus came to earth, put on human flesh, and was crucified on the cross to save us. It was there in the Garden of Gethsemane that mankind ultimately rejected Him.

Jesus was spat on, mocked, ridiculed, beaten, and flogged with a whip. Roman soldiers thrust a crown of thorns on His head and forced Him to carry a cross to Golgotha. Nails were driven into His feet and hands (or wrists), securing Him to the cross.

Soldiers hurled insults and scoffed at Him as He suffered agonizing pain and struggled to breathe. Finally, Jesus said, "It is finished," and bowed His head and gave up His spirit (John 19:30). A soldier pierced His side with a spear, confirming His death. Jesus' body was wrapped in linen and laid in a new tomb in the garden.

The next day, soldiers sealed the tomb and posted a guard. Three days later, Mary Magdalene and the other Mary visited the tomb. When they arrived, they saw an angel come down from Heaven and roll back the stone. The angel said, "He is not here; he has risen" (Matthew 28:6).

• • • OUR ONLY HOPE • • •

Oh, what a glorious hope we have in Jesus! The tomb is empty! Death has been defeated. The Gospel is not just good news but *amazing* news for those who accept God's free gift of salvation. But how do we do that and become saved?

My friend, salvation is shockingly simple: Believe in your heart that God raised Jesus from the dead and confess with your mouth that "Jesus is Lord" (Romans 10:9–10). That's it. Nothing more, nothing less. God is a merciful God who longs for *all* to be saved (1 Timothy 2:4).

But because He gave us free will, not all people will choose to believe in Him. The sad reality is that some parents will never get to meet their babies in Heaven. Not because their babies aren't there (I share biblical reasons why I believe babies are saved in chapter 5), but because the baby's parents do not place their faith in Christ. It's a heartbreaking reality that should spur us to urgently share the hope of the Gospel with everyone we can.

Jesus is the hope-filled solution to our seemingly hopeless situation. He is the only One who can save us from our sins and assure us an eternity in Heaven. Jesus is *the* Way, *the* Truth, and *the* Life. No one comes to the Father except through Him (John 14:6). There is no other option, no other religion, no other name by which we can be saved (Acts 4:12).

Jesus is the only cure for death, giving us what we so desperately seek: reunion with our babies. His empty tomb is the hope for our empty wombs. And the best news of the Gospel? We will not only be reunited with our babies but *reunited forever!* The separation we currently face is only temporary. Our reunion will last for all of eternity.

"Amazing Grace" is one of my favorite hymns. I love the last stanza:

> When we've been there ten thousand years,
> Bright shining as the sun,
> We've no less days to sing God's praise
> Than when we first begun.[2]

After ten thousand years of being with our children, we will have no fewer days to spend with them than when we first began! Can you imagine that? The short time we carried them in our wombs or held them in our arms on earth will pale in comparison to the endless years we will have together in Heaven (if time is even measured in years in Heaven).

There will be no end to time, and we will never fear being separated from them again! In Heaven, your title of "grieving mom" will be no more. It will be a distant memory of your earthly past. You will no longer need to look at ultrasound or remembrance photos and wonder what your baby looks like—instead, you will be gazing upon their sweet face forever.

Gone are the days of seeing your child's name on memorial items; instead, you'll be saying their name in their presence. No more holding onto the clothes you wished they could wear; you will be holding their hand and exploring the wonders of Heaven together.

Momma, I want you to see your baby again. But even more than that, I want you to know the One who made your baby—who made you! I want you to experience His love, mercy, and peace. I'm convinced there is nothing the world could offer you that would be better than Christ.

The Gospel changes everything. If you haven't yet accepted Christ, there is no better time than now. He will radically transform you, making you a new creation (2 Corinthians 5:17). You don't have to come to Him clean. There is no sin you committed in the past or are struggling with now that Jesus won't forgive if you repent and believe in Him.

John proclaimed that the blood of Jesus "purifies us from *all* sin" (1 John 1:7, emphasis added). What sins do you need God's grace to cover? Promiscuity in high school? Wild ways in college? A secret sin or addiction? I don't know of anyone who isn't ashamed of something in their past, including me. We all struggle with *something* because of our sinful nature.

Friend, you are not too far gone, too dirty, or too messed up. Jesus came to save sinners. He died for *you*. As far as the east is from the west, so far has He removed your transgressions from you (Psalm 103:12). *Nothing* can separate you from His love (Romans 8:38–39).

I wish I could look you in the eyes and tell you this: Jesus loves you, for the Bible tells me so. That song, "Jesus Loves Me"—which we sang at Bridget's funeral—isn't just for children. It's for you and me. He loves you so much and longs to have a relationship with you. You are His daughter, and He delights in you. Invite Him into your heart, and He will never leave you. Jesus is your only hope!

Prayers to Heaven

Jesus, thank You for the Gospel. We are so grateful that You took our place and died for our sins. Without You, we would be eternally separated from You. Thank You for forgiving us and washing us clean. Because of Your sacrifice, we will one day stand righteous before Your Father and enter Heaven for eternity. We praise You for making a way for us to be with You—and our babies—forever!

Truth to Cling To

Mark 16:15; Luke 24:45–49; Romans 1:16; 2 Corinthians 5:21; Galatians 1; Ephesians 1:13–14; 1 Peter 3:18–22

Time with Jesus

1. Being physically separated from our babies is excruciatingly painful. Handing Bridget over to the funeral home was the hardest moment for me. When did you feel the "sting of death"? Which moment felt the most final?

2. Read The Simple Gospel chart (appendix 2, page 255), and write a single sentence summarizing each of the four parts of the metanarrative of Scripture: *Creation, Fall, Redemption,* and *Restoration.* Then, condense the Gospel into one sentence. I've provided an example in your *CIH Guided Journal.*

3. Jesus saved us from an eternity in Hell apart from Him. Write a prayer of gratitude for His gift of salvation and thank Him for the hope He gives us to spend eternity

with Him and our babies in Heaven. If you haven't yet placed your faith in Jesus, reflect on what is holding you back.

HEALING STEPS

1. We cannot understand the Gospel's significance without knowing the full extent of what Jesus endured on our behalf. Read one of the accounts of His crucifixion in the Gospels that can be found in Matthew 27, Mark 15, Luke 23, or John 19.

2. Is there a past or present sin pulling you away from Him? Confess your sins to Him, and let Him forgive you. List your sins on paper, then shred it, knowing Jesus has already paid your debt in full.

3. The Gospel changes everything! If you've never accepted Jesus as your Lord and Savior, now is a great time to make the best decision of your life. If you confess with your mouth and believe in your heart that God raised Jesus from the dead, He will save you (see Romans 10:9–10 on page 67).

4

A Firm Foundation

WHEN YOU WRESTLE WITH DOUBTS

> I waited patiently for the LORD;
>   He turned to me and heard my cry.
> He lifted me out of the slimy pit,
>   out of the mud and mire;
> he set my feet on a rock
>   and gave me a firm place to stand.
>
> Psalm 40:1–2

Two days after Bridget was born, Matt and I visited the funeral home to hold her one more time before she would be placed in her casket. We brought my mint green blankie from childhood and bundled her, inside her cradle, in the larger blanket.

Matt and I took turns reading letters to her, singing songs, and kissing her sweet face—our lips enveloping her little button nose and tiny lips in one kiss. Holding her again, for the last time in my earthly life, brought a swell of emotions *and* hormones.

That day, my milk came in with full force—a brutal reminder that my body was prepared to nourish a life that wasn't here anymore. My breast tissue was engorged, throbbing with milk I didn't need. Not knowing what to do, I texted a friend who had experienced stillbirth.

She gave me advice on how to dry up my milk, but I'll never forget something she said: "Your milk coming in after your baby died is like getting kicked when you're down." Yes, that's exactly how it felt. I took a hot shower to relieve the intense physical pain.

Standing naked and vulnerable in the shower, I burst into uncontrollable tears as milk seeped from where Bridget should have been latched. I knelt on the shower floor as hot water pelted my back. I cried out to God: "I miss her so much. I just want her back. I would do anything to be pregnant with her right now! My whole body aches for her. *God, I can't do this!*"

Absolutely *everything* felt unbearably empty: my womb, my arms, our home. I longed for her to be safe in my belly and wondered if I would survive the crushing weight of my sorrow. If you've ever had to flush your toilet after experiencing an early miscarriage or leave the hospital without the precious baby once nestled inside your womb, you know this kind of intense anguish.

As the nursery you prepared for them sits painfully empty, the reality of their death sets in—and so do all the questions: *Is Jesus really who He said He is? If so, is Heaven real? How can I be sure my baby is there? Will I ever be with them again?*

In chapter 2, we discussed how these questions can cause a crisis of faith. In chapter 3, we talked about how the Gospel changes everything. But what if you *do* believe in God, Jesus, and Heaven, yet you wrestle with doubts? Friend, if you do, you are not alone.

Personally speaking, I wish God would split the sky for a second so I could see the glory of Heaven with my own two eyes. If I could see Bridget there, happy in Paradise, it would change my perspective for the rest of my life. I'd have peace about her being there, and it'd be easier to focus the rest of my days on my journey to my Heavenly Home.

I also wish I could meet Jesus face-to-face and talk to Him right now! *Then* I'd know that He is real and that my beliefs are true! Oh, wouldn't it be so much easier to follow Christ if we could actually see Him? Have you ever had similar thoughts?

Unfortunately, as we learned in the last chapter, we have temporarily lost the privilege of walking with Him in a physical way on earth due to the Fall. Instead, our relationship with Him is based on *faith*, which is "confidence in what we hope for and assurance about what *we do not see*" (Hebrews 11:1, emphasis added).

We cannot see God. We have not met Jesus in the flesh. We have not been to Heaven. Believing in their existence requires us to have faith. Paul declared, "Therefore we are always confident and know that as long as we are at home in the body we are away from the Lord. For we live by faith, not by sight" (2 Corinthians 5:6–7).

How do we live by faith when we are taught that "seeing is believing"? Maybe you want to believe in Jesus, but you wish you had more proof that He's real. Can you relate to doubting Thomas? He was one of Jesus' apostles and insisted, "Unless I see the nail marks in his hands and put my finger where the nails were, and put my hand into his side, I will not believe" (John 20:25).

• • • LUNATIC, LIAR, OR LORD • • •

Jesus Christ is the most renowned person in history. His birth divided time in history (BC to AD). The Bible, a testament to His life, has been translated into more than seven hundred languages, reaching tribes and nations across the earth.

The Bible is the world's bestselling book of all time[1] and is the bestselling book of the year every year.[2] About eighty million

Bibles are sold annually, and it is estimated that five to seven billion Bibles have been printed.[3]

There are churches in every country and on every other street corner in the United States. Major holidays are centered on Jesus' birth and Resurrection. Very few people—not even most atheists—would debate the fact that a man named Jesus existed and died on a cross. His life and death were well documented and witnessed.

However, the debate revolves around whether Jesus truly was who He claimed to be and whether His Resurrection actually happened. During His time on earth, Jesus publicly proclaimed Himself to be the long-awaited Messiah (Mark 14:61–62)—the promised Savior who would save the Jews (and the world) from their sins. His bold assertion was either blasphemous or true.

In *Mere Christianity*, C. S. Lewis declared that Jesus must have been a lunatic, a liar, or the Lord to make such a claim.[4] To profess to be God in the flesh, He either had to be deranged, deceitful, or indeed who He said He was: the Son of God. There is an entire branch of theology dedicated to defending the truth of Christianity called *apologetics*.[5] If you struggle with doubts or want to defend your faith, I encourage you to read an apologetics book.

We should "always be prepared to *give an answer* to everyone who asks you to *give the reason* for the hope that you have" (1 Peter 3:15, emphasis added). Because my book is focused on the promise of seeing our babies again in Heaven, through faith in Jesus, I feel it is important to tell you why I believe His claims were true.

Since I am encouraging you to hinge all your hope on Jesus, I want you to know why He is real and trustworthy. Maybe you're like Thomas, and you want proof of His Resurrection. But you can't physically see His nail-scarred hands or touch His side. You weren't in the upper room when Jesus appeared to His disciples after His death. So, what is the next best thing to seeing it for yourself? Eyewitness accounts!

To believe Jesus rose from the dead, we need to rely on the accounts of the people who saw Him alive *after* His crucifixion. If we only had the empty tomb—without reports of His post-death appearances—we would have to *presume* Jesus defeated death. If this were the case, there would be reason for skepticism. Was His body stolen? Did somebody move Him? Thankfully, our faith is not based merely on speculation.

We have numerous and credible eyewitness accounts of Jesus' Resurrection. Over five hundred people saw Jesus living and breathing after His death (1 Corinthians 15:5–7). These were not only random people, but some were His closest friends and followers who had witnessed His death and then saw Him alive again. Over a span of forty days, Jesus "gave many convincing proofs that he was alive" (Acts 1:3).

So why do I believe in Jesus? There are many reasons, but in my opinion, the most convincing proof is the radical life change of Jesus' disciples. Their testimonies, chronicled in the New Testament, attest to the validity of Jesus' claims. Their extreme boldness and unwavering courage in the face of persecution provide compelling evidence that validates the truth of what they saw and believed about their friend Jesus.

Imagine being in the sandals of a disciple who walked with Jesus. They witnessed Him perform countless miracles. I've listed some of these incredible experiences in appendix 3. After Jesus' death and Resurrection, however, His twelve disciples were greatly persecuted for sharing their faith in Jesus.

In addition, Paul—who had a personal encounter with Jesus on the road to Damascus and converted from being a *persecutor* of Christians to a *follower* of Christ—was shipwrecked, beaten, chained, flogged, and on the brink of death time and time again. He detailed his sufferings in 2 Corinthians 11, writing, "Five times I received from the Jews the forty lashes minus one" (v. 24).

According to tradition and the writings of early church historian Eusebius, Paul was eventually beheaded at the direction of Emperor Nero in Rome,[6] possibly in AD 67. Peter, the disciple who denied Jesus three times, was crucified in Rome. Also according to tradition and extrabiblical accounts, Peter requested to be crucified upside down (on an inverted cross) because he felt unworthy to die in the same manner as Jesus.[7]

The rest of the disciples, excluding John, died as martyrs in gruesome deaths. Why would they risk their lives for a lie or hoax? They were willing to be persecuted, tortured, and even killed for what they believed to be true: Their friend was the Son of God. The uncompromising loyalty of the men who knew Jesus on earth and saw Him alive after His death is one of the greatest reasons I believe in Jesus today. I pray their testimony and willingness to endure trials for the sake of the risen Christ would strengthen your faith too.

• • • STRONGEST FAITH • • •

I have loved the name Bridget Faith since I was in eighth grade. When I started dating Matt, I told him that if we were to get married, I wanted to name our first daughter Bridget Faith. He agreed, which further solidified that he was the one for me. Actually, we both knew on our very first date that we wanted to marry each other!

As Matt left our bowling and dinner date, he texted his friend, "She's the one," and I told my parents that I had met the man I was going to marry. In May 2014, we were married in a beautiful ceremony underneath a wooden arbor my dad and Matt had built together. Our wedding theme was "Grace and Redemption" because God had redeemed both of us from the pain and betrayal of past relationships and graciously given us the gift of each other.

Two weeks after a wonderful honeymoon in St. Lucia, I got puppy fever, and we drove to Texas to pick up a golden retriever that we named Braxton. (Can you tell we like BR names?) We were acclimating to married life with a cute but very ornery puppy when I noticed that my period was late. I decided to take a pregnancy test, which, to my surprise, was positive. Just one month after our wedding, we found out we were expecting a honeymoon baby!

It was a shock to me because I had always assumed I would struggle with infertility, given my history with polycystic ovary syndrome (PCOS). We were elated and grateful that God had blessed us with a baby. Days later, we went to a bookstore and bought *What to Expect When You're Expecting* and *The Expectant Father*.

After my first OB appointment at eight weeks, we took home a video of our baby's heartbeat. We then shared the happy news with our families and started to plan for our future as a family of three. Each Friday, I took pictures of my growing bump. Life was good.

However, our excitement came to a sudden halt at thirteen weeks and four days into my pregnancy. I was at work, in my former job as a speech-language pathologist, when I started experiencing heavy bleeding. I ran to the bathroom and started crying as blood soaked through my dress pants. One of my co-workers, a close friend, came into the stall with me, wrapped her sweatshirt around my waist, and immediately drove me to the nearest emergency room.

When we got there, her sweatshirt was soaked in blood, and I was certain I must be miscarrying. Matt and my mom quickly met us in the emergency room, partitioned off by thin curtains. I lay on the bed, terrified and worried about our baby. The doctor came in and did a sonogram. We saw our sweet baby sucking their thumb, which relieved our fears that he or she had died due to the bleeding. But what was all the dark space filling the screen?

The doctor pointed to the black crescent shape filling the white portion of the sonogram and said, "This is a subchorionic hemorrhage. It is filling about 50 percent of your womb. There is about a 50 percent chance you will miscarry. The best thing you can do is go on bed rest, but other than that, there's nothing else you can do."

So, we went home, and thus began my days of bed rest. Honestly, they were some of the hardest days of my life. I spent the majority of my time in bed or on the couch, trying to take it as easy as possible. The bleeding continued every single day, and I grew weary from changing so many pads. I felt abandoned by God, and I struggled with my faith.

At nineteen weeks, we had an appointment with our high-risk specialty doctor. We received more bad news: My hemorrhage was growing larger and was now abrupting the placenta—tearing it away from the uterine wall. Because of this, our baby was diagnosed with intrauterine growth restriction (IUGR) as he/she was measuring several weeks behind.

Our hearts shattered as we looked at our baby's sweet profile in the updated sonogram picture we were given. We both cried on our way home, holding the envelope that contained our baby's gender. We had planned to host a gender reveal party the following day but were now unsure if our baby would ever come home with us. Should we cancel the party? I wasn't in a good place emotionally, but Matt encouraged me to proceed with our plans.

He said, "No matter what happens, we will never regret celebrating our baby's life." I am so glad I listened to him because he was right. Opening the box of pink balloons in our front yard and watching them drift off into the sky was an incredibly surreal experience. We were having a girl!

Our friends and family came over, wearing pink or blue, and we burst open pink and purple confetti in our dining room to see their faces light up with delight. Then Matt and I cut a cake to reveal pink frosting inside. My friend photographed everything, documenting one of the best days of my life. I wrote in my journal: "I wish I could have lived in this moment forever. It was pure joy. For one second, we forgot about all the medical problems and just enjoyed the moment together."

But that night, Matt and I had an important decision to discuss. Now that we knew our baby was a girl and doctors didn't expect her to survive, would we still name her Bridget Faith? We both prayed about it in the days that followed. I wrestled with surrendering her name. What if we named her Bridget, and she died? We wouldn't get to raise a daughter by that name.

However, one week before her birth, the Lord confirmed to me that her name was Bridget Faith, regardless of whether she would live here or in Heaven. Bridget means *strength*, so together with her middle name, her full name means *strongest faith*. It was the perfect name for her; she was a small but strong little girl. But also because her life and death *strengthened my faith*.

I didn't "lose" her name. In fact, her name has left my lips every single day since she was born. Because I lead a ministry in her memory, thousands of people know her name. But most importantly, her name lives on because she is an eternal being. Just like your precious son or daughter. The name you chose for him or her will live on forever.

And if you haven't chosen a name for your baby, it's never too late to decide on one. Even if it's been years since they went to Heaven, it can be incredibly healing and validating to name your baby. I've personally walked with many mommas who have chosen to name their babies even years later.

You can still name your baby even if you weren't very far along in your pregnancy and you didn't know their gender. Many moms choose a neutral name or one based on the gender they thought their baby might be. Also, don't feel ashamed if you've decided not to name your baby. It's okay to refer to them as Baby (Your Last Name). I am confident that God knows their name, and one day, in Heaven, you will too.

• • • CHRIST THE SOLID ROCK • • •

Coming back to the meaning of Bridget's name, I want to close this chapter with what it means to have "strongest faith" in the midst of grief and loss. My friend, you may have realized by now that your baby's death is not something you can separate from the rest of your life. Grief affects every part of you, including your faith, marriage, family, friendships, work, health, and even your day-to-day activities.

In the same way, your faith also influences everything about you. Your beliefs about life, also known as your worldview, dictate how you perceive God and your circumstances. Everything you experience is filtered through the lens of your worldview, which seeks to answer five important questions. I've listed them below, and I've rewritten the questions in the right column to be more specific for a grieving mother.

	Worldview Question[8]	Grieving Mother Question
Origin	Where did I come from?	Where did my baby come from?
Identity	Who am I?	Who is my baby?
Meaning	What is my purpose?	What is my baby's purpose? What is my purpose now that I have lost my baby?
Morality	How should I live?	How does God want me to live in response to my grief?
Destiny	What happens when I die?	What happened when my baby died? Will I be reunited with them when I die? Where will we live together?

How you answer these questions will shape everything about your life:

- The choices you make
- The things you do
- The words you say
- The thoughts you think
- The information you consume
- The relationships you keep
- The values you hold
- The outlook you have of the future

Your worldview will also play a significant role in how you heal from the loss of your baby. There are two ways to heal: the world's way or the Word's way. Only the latter will lead to true and lasting healing. For that reason, I've written this book based on the *biblical worldview* I hold, which is founded on the Word of God and rooted in the hope of Christ.

When Thomas asked Jesus if he could touch His side and feel the holes in His hands, Jesus allowed him to do so. But then He said, "Stop doubting and believe" (John 20:27). Friends, I do not want to minimize our struggles with doubts, but similar to the plea of the apostles to the Lord in Luke 17:5, we need to ask God to "Increase our faith!"

Jesus is alive and now seated at the right hand of the Father (Hebrews 10:12–13). He is our steadfast hope and our firm foundation. As David proclaimed,

> The LORD is my rock, my fortress and my deliverer;
> my God is my rock, in whom I take refuge,
> my shield and the horn of my salvation, my
> stronghold.
>
> Psalm 18:2

In the parable of the builders in Matthew 7, Jesus compares two men, one who built his house on a rock and another who built his house on sand. The rock represents a solid, unchanging foundation, while the sand symbolizes a shifting, unstable base. Jesus said that whoever hears His words and does them will be like the wise man who built his house on the rock (v. 24–25). When the floods came and the winds blew, the house remained standing.

Not so for the foolish man who built his house on the sand. When adverse weather came, his house came crashing down (v. 27). I want to draw a parallel for us as grieving moms. When the floodwaters (of sorrow) and winds (of grief) rage and beat against our house (heart), will we be able to withstand the storm? The answer is a resounding yes if we anchor our heart's hope in the unshakable love of Christ. I love these lines written by Robert Mote, from the hymn *My Hope Is Built on Nothing Less*:

> My hope is built on nothing less
> Than Jesus' blood and righteousness;
> I dare not trust the sweetest frame,
> But wholly lean on Jesus' name.
>
> On Christ, the solid Rock, I stand;
> All other ground is sinking sand;
> All other ground is sinking sand.[9]

And praise God, our firm foundation of faith isn't some brainwashed, wishful-thinking kind of hope. This is the bet-your-life-on-it, cling-with-all-your-might kind of hope, secured in the real-life, really-did-happen Resurrection of Jesus. When we take our last breath on this earth, we will be eternally glad we placed our faith in Him—for at that moment, our faith will finally become sight as we gaze upon His glory in the splendor of Heaven!

PRAYERS TO HEAVEN

Jesus, when our lives feel like they're falling apart, You are our firm foundation, the solid Rock on which we stand. We believe You are who You said You are: the promised Messiah and the Son of God. Thank You for Your disciples and their brave testimonies. We desire to trust You with our whole hearts, knowing that You personally and intimately understand our pain and grief. Help us overcome any disbelief or doubts we have. Increase and strengthen our faith. We love You, Jesus. Amen.

TRUTH TO CLING TO

Isaiah 28:16; Matthew 16:15–17; Mark 9:23–24; John 1:14–41; James 1:5–6; 1 Corinthians 3:11; Ephesians 2:20

TIME WITH JESUS

1. Are you struggling with doubts? Where are you in your faith journey right now? Identify any areas of disbelief and surrender them to the Lord.
2. Your worldview matters and will shape how you heal. Look at the chart on page 88. Write down your beliefs regarding the five important questions: origin, meaning, identity, morality, and destiny. If you hold a biblical worldview, jot down Scripture to support your answers.
3. Defending your faith is important. If someone asked you why you believe in Jesus, what would you tell them?

HEALING STEPS

1. Looking for more proof to believe in Jesus? I recommend that you read a Christian apologetics book, listen to believers' testimonies on podcasts, or spend time diving into the Word.
2. Jesus' Resurrection and the loyalty of His disciples are the top reasons I believe in Him. Look at the chart in appendix 3 on page 257. Read a Scripture verse from each section and imagine what it must have been like to witness Jesus' life firsthand.

3. Listen to *My Hope Is Built on Nothing Less* (in some hymnals, it may be called *On Christ the Solid Rock*). If you feel comfortable, lift your hands in surrender and praise Him for who He is and what He has done for you.

5

Heaven on Earth

WHEN YOU WONDER WHERE YOUR BABY IS

> What no eye has seen, no ear has heard,
> and no human heart has conceived—
> God has prepared these things for those who love
> Him.
>
> 1 Corinthians 2:9 CSB

Imagine the most beautiful place you've ever visited. Close your eyes and let your mind paint its landscape across the back of your eyelids. Is it the vast peaks of snow-capped mountains or the serene waters of your favorite lake? Is it the ocean's crashing waves or a breathtaking sunset in your hometown?

Draw in a deep breath and take a few minutes to escape there. When you've fully experienced your special place and locked in your mental image, open your eyes. Where did you go? I chose to get away to a small island in the Caribbean Sea called Saint Lucia.

On the beach, I am rocking back and forth on a cushioned swing bed, fastened by ropes to a tree that bends overhead. The tree's crisp green leaves provide shade for the day. The tree is planted in the soft sand, mere feet from the calm sea. I can hear the waves gently lapping up onto the shore. Clear aqua waters merge into a blue sky, with puffy white clouds contrasting against the lush green mountains poking up in the distance.

It's easy for me to imagine this tropical paradise because it was where Matt and I went on our honeymoon in May 2014. We stayed at a resort, but the nature around us seemed untouched by mankind. Surrounded by the beauty of God's Creation, my soul could rest there. The burdens of everyday life melted away as we swung in the breeze, tan legs kissed by the warm sun and lungs full of fresh ocean air.

In my everyday life in Kansas, I'm usually an on-the-go, can't-sit-and-relax type of person. Spending leisure time feels like being lazy to me. My mentality of "scratch one thing off and add two more things" to my to-do list usually controls me.

Amid such gorgeous landscapes, my rushed personality finally relaxed. I felt safe and at peace. And it was here on this island that we unexpectedly conceived the miracle of life—our first child! Yes, God chose for Bridget's life to begin in Saint Lucia, my little piece of Heaven on earth.

• • • DISTORTED VIEWS • • •

I believe the most magnificent place you've ever witnessed on earth is merely a glimpse of the majesty that awaits us in Heaven. Though we have the beautiful backdrop of God's Creation all around us, it's hard to fathom the true splendor of Heaven—a place untouched by sin and corruption.

Do you ever feel skeptical about how incredible Heaven will be? Perhaps you grew up thinking as I did, that Heaven was an obscure, remote place that was ethereal and, dare I say, boring. It would be a good place, but it wouldn't be somewhere fun or desirable.

I envisioned myself becoming like a programmed robot forced to float on the clouds and sing "Holy, Holy, Holy" in unison with the angels forever. It's not that I *don't* want to worship God—I *do* want to worship Him for all of eternity! But deep down, I want Heaven—and even worship—to feel familiar. I want to feel like myself as I freely praise Him.

In many ways, the abstract concepts I adopted when I was younger made me think I would somehow lose my identity in Heaven. I wondered if I would feel homesick for earth while living in Heaven as if I had left my true self behind. Who would I be if I no longer had unique preferences, desires, fascinations, or strengths? What would I do if I couldn't do my favorite things?

Would Heaven be Heaven if I couldn't spend time with family and friends, learn new things, explore, travel, and use my talents to serve Christ and others? Thankfully, my childhood views are far from the truth! We have nothing to worry about because the monotonous floating on clouds and playing harps for eternity version of Heaven is not biblical.

Scripture's depiction of Heaven is quite the contrary! In fact, it is so much better than we could ever hope or imagine; just thinking about it makes me homesick for Heaven! In his book *Heaven*, Randy Alcorn compares what we assume about Heaven to what the Bible actually says about it.

Before you read the chart below, adapted from Alcorn's book,[1] take a moment to reflect on how you currently envision Heaven. I pray God's Word will give you a renewed perspective and eager anticipation for Heaven!

What We Assume about Heaven	What the Bible Says about Heaven
Non-Earth	New Earth
Unfamiliar; otherworldly	Familiar; earthly
Disembodied	Resurrected (embodied)
Foreign	Home

continued

What We Assume about Heaven	What the Bible Says about Heaven
Leaving favorite things behind	Retaining the good; finding the best ahead
Nothing to do, floating on the clouds	A God to worship and serve, purposeful work to accomplish, friends to enjoy
Boring	Fascinating
Absence of the terrible (but the presence of little we desire)	Presence of the wonderful (everything we desire and nothing we don't)

Some content taken from *Heaven* by Randy Alcorn. Copyright © 2004. Used by permission of Tyndale House Publishers. All rights reserved.

⊹ ⊹ ⊹ TWO HEAVENS ⊹ ⊹ ⊹

Did you notice Heaven will be earthly? Does that mean *this* earth will become Heaven? No, there are two Heavens—the *current Heaven*, which is temporary, and the *coming Heaven*, which is eternal.

The current Heaven is where believers' souls—in the past and present—go when they take their final breath. Paul told us that to be absent from the body is to be present with the Lord (2 Corinthians 5:8). Jesus assured us that those who believe in Him will immediately be in His presence upon death. Remember what He told the repentant criminal on the cross next to Him? "Today you will be with me in paradise" (Luke 23:43 ESV).

Paradise! What an incredible word for Jesus to use to describe Heaven. Doesn't it make you think it will be beautiful beyond imagination? And though it is a spiritual place, it must also be a physical place. This mystery is hard for us to understand now, but it will be revealed to us one day.

But for now, because the Resurrection of believers has not yet happened, those in the current Heaven (including our babies) are temporarily disembodied. In chapter 7, I will explain how God made us in three parts: body, soul, and spirit. When a believer dies, their soul and spirit depart from their earthly body as they enter Heaven. At a later time appointed by God, Jesus will resurrect their earthly body and give them their glorified body.

In 1 Corinthians 15, Paul describes this incredible transformation: "The splendor of the heavenly bodies is one kind, and the splendor of the earthly bodies is another" (v. 40), and "So will it be with the resurrection of the dead. The body that is sown is perishable, it is raised imperishable" (v. 42).

I will discuss the sequence of these events in more detail in chapter 14, but after Jesus returns and reigns for a thousand years, we will live in our glorified bodies on the New Earth, also known as the New Heaven. We learn about it in the final book of the Bible, Revelation. God gave the apostle John a view of the End Times, culminating in Jesus' Second Coming.

Around the year AD 95, John penned his vivid visions while on the island of Patmos, where the Romans had exiled him for preaching the Gospel:

> Then I saw "a new heaven and a new earth," for the first heaven and the first earth had passed away, and there was no longer any sea. I saw the Holy City, the new Jerusalem, coming down out of heaven from God, prepared as a bride beautifully dressed for her husband. And I heard a loud voice from the throne saying, "Look! God's dwelling place is now among the people, and he will dwell with them. They will be his people, and God himself will be with them and be their God.
>
> Revelation 21:1–3

Based on John's writings, we can see that there is both a *first* Heaven and a *New* Heaven. The first Heaven is the current Heaven—a temporary place where souls reside until the Resurrection. But isn't it so exciting to know that a *New* Heaven and *New* Earth are coming? I don't know about you, but I cannot wait for the Resurrection, when Jesus will empty our babies' graves and resurrect their bodies!

If you chose cremation for your baby's remains, Jesus will collect their ashes and make them whole again. Remember, God first created man "from the dust of the ground" (Genesis 2:7). Babies who were buried will also return to dust (Genesis 3:19). Dust will be what He uses to make our babies whole again.

The New Earth will be our forever home. It will feel familiar, but it will be absolute perfection because sin and death will not exist there. You will hold your sweet baby and never fear being separated again. Be encouraged by my favorite Bible verse, Revelation 21:4: "He will wipe every tear from their eyes. There will be no more death or mourning or crying or pain, for the old order of things has passed away."

As for our current earth? God will destroy it by fire. "The day of the Lord will come like a thief. The heavens will disappear with a roar; the elements will be destroyed by fire, and the earth and everything done in it will be laid bare" (2 Peter 3:10).

There will be no more wars, diseases, disasters, deception, corruption, or injustice. Death will be gone forever, and Jesus will reign in perfect justice. We will live in unity because sin will no longer divide us. Jesus will right every wrong, and we will live fully and wholly in God's presence. We will lack and want nothing!

• • • THE BEST PLACE TO BE • • •

One of my greatest comforts is knowing Bridget is safe in Heaven, protected against the brokenness of this world. She left the comfort of my womb and entered into the presence of Jesus. As our pastor proclaimed at her funeral, Bridget went from the safest place to the safest place. All she ever knew was love and joy; what better life could she have had?

Bridget will never know what it feels like to have her heart broken. No one will lie to, betray, reject, or abandon her. She will never experience anxiety or depression. She won't be tempted to sin or suffer its unpleasant consequences. Bridget will never feel the weight of shame, guilt, or regret. She will never deal with relational tension, health ailments, financial problems, work stress, or a host of other difficulties one could face in this life.

There is a book in the Bible about a man named Job, a righteous man who loved God and was blameless before Him. However, Satan believed Job only obeyed God because He had blessed him. Satan suggested that God remove His protection from Job and destroy everything he had. So God allowed Satan to kill his livestock and all his sons and daughters.

But even after enduring such grief, Job maintained his integrity and faith in God. So Satan afflicted him with painful sores all over his body. After Job experienced this excruciating suffering, he cursed the day he was born. In his distress, he asked God, "Why was I not hidden away in the ground like a *stillborn* child, like an infant who never saw the light of day?" (Job 3:16, emphasis added).

Never saw the light of day. As a bereaved mom, this statement initially bothered me. It saddened me to think Bridget had never seen the sun or experienced life on this earth. How could someone wish they were stillborn? But, when we contrast this earth's brokenness with Heaven's perfection, I can understand Job's perspective better.

Our babies are happy and whole, living abundant lives in a perfect Paradise. We are the ones stuck living on this broken earth, enduring endless trials and pain. If God gave us even a glimpse of the glory our babies are experiencing, we wouldn't want them to come back to this sin-stained earth. In fact, *we* would want to go straight *there* and bypass the troubles of this world.

• • • WHERE IS THE CURRENT HEAVEN? • • •

Contrary to popular belief, Scripture provides clear indications about the location of Heaven. It is not some distant, mystical realm but a place above us. The Bible is replete with references that unequivocally state Heaven is directly above the earth, while Hell is beneath it.

The Old Testament writers, under the divine inspiration of the Holy Spirit, provide these accounts of Heaven's location in relation to the earth (emphases added):

> **Moses:** "Even if you have been banished to the most distant land *under the heavens,* from there the LORD your God will gather you and bring you back" (Deuteronomy 30:4); "[God,] look *down from heaven,* your holy dwelling place" (Deuteronomy 26:15).

> **Joshua:** "For the LORD your God is God *in heaven above and on the earth below*" (Joshua 2:11).

> **David:** "God looks *down from heaven* on all mankind" (Psalm 53:2).

> **Solomon:** "LORD, the God of Israel, there is no God like you *in heaven above or on earth below*" (1 Kings 8:23).

> **Isaiah:** "This is what the LORD says: 'Heaven is my throne, and the *earth is my footstool*' (Isaiah 66:1).

It brings me great joy to know Bridget is above me. When I look at the sky, I know she is right *up there* with God. I don't know exactly how many miles above us, but when I fly on an airplane, I know, Scripturally speaking, I am closer to Heaven than when I was on the ground. On a flight to Texas, after Bridget went to Heaven, I wrote in my journal: "I am as close to Bridget as I can be."

• • • WILL OUR BABIES BE ANGELS IN HEAVEN? • • •

In the pregnancy and infant loss community, people commonly refer to babies in Heaven as "angel babies." You've probably heard someone say, "God must have needed another angel," or "Now you have an angel looking over you." Though some moms may believe their babies become angels when they die, most moms use this phrase without intending to make an inaccurate theological statement.

Our babies do *not* become angels, and that's a very good thing! God made angels as separate beings to serve specific roles in His Kingdom, such as fighting battles in the spiritual realm and delivering messages to earth (Hebrews 1:13–14; Luke 24:39). Humans are distinct from angels in that we have physical bodies and will participate in a bodily resurrection (1 Thessalonians 4:16–17). God intentionally made us in His image to be His children.

Paul declared, "If we are [God's] children, then we are heirs—heirs of God and co-heirs with Christ" (Romans 8:17). As co-heirs, we are greater than the angels! Paul told us we will even judge the angels (1 Corinthians 6:3). Thankfully, our babies will remain humans in Heaven, just as God created them.

• • • HOW OLD WILL OUR BABIES BE IN HEAVEN? • • •

When daydreaming about seeing Bridget in Heaven, I sometimes envision her as the tiny thirteen-ounce baby I once held on earth. Other times, I imagine her as a full-term newborn infant, the size I had expected her to be if she had been born on her due date. And once in a while, I picture myself running on streets of gold holding the hand of a long-haired brunette, green-eyed little girl.

It's natural to wonder about our babies' appearance in Heaven. Yet, we simply don't have all the details. Scripture doesn't provide a clear answer about people's age in Heaven or whether age is even measured there. We will be living outside of the confines of time, so we can't definitively say whether our babies will be infants, children, or even adults when we reunite with them.

We also don't know if our babies will grow or age over eternity. I've wondered if we will see them at different stages of life or if they will remain at one constant age. Though I wish God addressed this particular topic in the Bible, He has not. He has chosen to remain silent. We cannot speculate one way or the other, which leaves room for us to have faith in the mystery.

While it's human nature to desire certainty, I find solace in trusting that God has a perfect plan for our children in Heaven. Because He is good, we can be confident His plan is better than we can imagine and will not disappoint us. Our babies are safe and secure in Jesus' loving arms. We will be overjoyed when we see them again—whatever form their bodies are in.

• • • HOW CAN I BE SURE BABIES GO TO HEAVEN? • • •

There are several reasons why many biblical scholars and Christians, including me, believe God allows babies to go to Heaven:

- Babies have not reached the age of accountability.
- Jesus loves children.
- God's character is good and just.
- There is a biblical precedent for babies going to Heaven.

The age of accountability is a debated topic in theological circles. At what age does God hold children or young adults accountable for their actions? At what point can a child fully understand the Gospel and choose to place their faith in Jesus? Some theologians believe the age of accountability is around thirteen, and others think it varies from child to child.

The Bible does not give us a specific age, but it does acknowledge that young children lack understanding and should not be judged for it. For example, Moses said Israel's children "who do not yet know good from bad" will take possession of the Promised Land. The rest of the evil generation, including their parents, would not get to step foot in it—only Joshua, Caleb, and the little ones of the nation would be allowed to enter (Deuteronomy 1:39).

In Jeremiah 19, when God addressed the detestable practice of sacrificing children on the altar of the foreign god Baal, He said, "They have filled this place with the blood of the innocent" (v. 4). Here we see that God views children as innocent, not deserving of death. We also see God's compassion for children in Jesus' actions during His time on earth.

In Mark 10 and Luke 18, we read that many people brought children to Jesus so He could place His hands on them. When His disciples rebuked them for doing so, Jesus was indignant and said, "Let the little children come to me, and do not hinder them, for the kingdom of God belongs to such as these. Truly I tell you, anyone who will not receive the kingdom of God like a little child will never enter it" (Mark 10:14–15; Luke 18:16–17).

Matthew 18:3 contains a similar message from Jesus: "Truly I tell you, unless you change and become like little children, you will never enter the kingdom of heaven." Jesus loves children. We also know His Kingdom is an upside-down one: The last will be first, and the first will be last (Matthew 20:16).

The least of these, such as tiny, precious unborn and newborn babies, may be considered the greatest in His Kingdom. We can trust that because God's character is good and just, He will take care of our babies—which are really His to begin with.

Lastly, there is a biblical precedent for babies going to Heaven in 2 Samuel 12. When King David's baby was sick, he fasted and prayed for his recovery. On the seventh day, his child died. At this point, David stopped fasting and no longer wept. His attendants questioned why he was no longer weeping.

David responded that he had been fasting so that "the Lord may be gracious to me and let the child live. But now that he is dead, why should I go on fasting? Can I bring him back again? I will go to him, but he will not return to me" (2 Samuel 12:22–23).

"I will go to him" implies that his baby went to Heaven and that David knows he will see him again one day. This story and statement—that God intentionally included in His Word—gives me confidence that our babies are in Heaven. Though we had longed to welcome our babies to earth, one day, they will welcome *us* to Heaven. Yes, we will surely *go to them!*

• • • CREATION RESTORED • • •

Let's revisit the place you pictured at the beginning of this chapter. Consider how much you currently enjoy your favorite spot in its *broken* state. Can you imagine what it will be like in its *restored* state? Try envisioning its beauty multiplied infinity to the infinite degree—the most significant number I could conjure up.

The wonder that awaits you on the New Earth will be beyond your wildest dreams! Read this chapter's opening verse again. Paul told us Heaven will be better than any human heart could ever conceive. I think we will see sights we can't fathom with our earthly minds and view vivid colors our eyes can't see on our present-day earth.

We will not need the sun because God Himself will be our light, and night will no longer exist (Revelation 21:23–25). Glistening streams and rivers as clear as glass will run through streets made of pure gold. The throne of God and the Tree of Life will be centered in the New Jerusalem (Revelation 22:1–4).

The New Earth will be the original Creation restored back to the Garden of Eden. Remember the metanarrative of Scripture (*Creation, Fall, Redemption,* and *Restoration*) in chapter 3/appendix 2? The New Earth is the ultimate destination of God's restoration plans! God is all about making things new. Think of all the *re* verbs associated with Him: *redemption, restoration, renewal, revival,* and *resurrection.* It's in His character to restore what He originally created.

The most exciting part about the New Earth is that we get to live there *with* Him! Sweet friend, be filled with anticipation. Jesus is alive, and He's coming back. A New Heaven is coming! It will be the earth God intended, and we will spend eternity there with our children. Until then, you can rest assured that they are basking in the glory of Jesus in the current Heaven.

PRAYERS TO HEAVEN

Jesus, thank You for the hope of Heaven! We are so grateful our babies are in a perfect Paradise far greater than we could ever imagine. Remind us that it is the best place they could be. Help us envision its splendor and wait in eager anticipation for our reunion with our babies in Heaven. One day, You will resurrect them, and we'll live together forever in our glorified bodies on the New Earth. We can't wait to live in a restored Eden with You and our children for eternity. Amen.

TRUTH TO CLING TO

Psalm 102:25–28; Ecclesiastes 3:11; Isaiah 25:6–9; Isaiah 65:17–18; 1 Corinthians 2:9; Philippians 3:20–21; 2 Peter 3:13

TIME WITH JESUS

1. Describe the place you envisioned at the beginning of this chapter. What makes it so beautiful? Why is it special to you?

2. Do you have distorted views of Heaven? Reflect on the beliefs you grew up with and how they influenced your perception of Heaven.

3. What excites you the most about Heaven? Did anything surprise you in this chapter, or did you learn anything new about Heaven?

HEALING STEPS

1. Studying Heaven through the lens of Scripture has increased my excitement about going there! Read Revelation 21–22 for a wonderful description of the New Earth.

2. Read *Heaven* by Randy Alcorn or another biblically based book on the topic. Be sure to always measure everything you read against Scripture.

3. On a clear night, grab a blanket and lie on your driveway or in your backyard. Gaze at the stars and fill your mind with thoughts of Heaven. Read Psalm 19:1 in the New King James Version. Spend time praying and being still in His presence.

6

For He Is Good

WHEN YOU QUESTION WHO GOD IS

Give thanks to the LORD, for he is good.
His love endures forever.

Psalm 136:1

I stood in the seemingly endless security line at the Atlanta airport, waiting for my turn to show my Kansas driver's license and remove my shoes for the TSA employees. I was coming home after visiting my friend, Amanda, who serves with me in Bridget's Cradles. As I zigzagged through the partitioned lines early that morning, I had nothing better to do than to people-watch.

I inched through the rows of people from all walks of life, varying in age, nationality, language, socioeconomic group, fashion style, hairstyle, and physique. As I examined each of their faces, I wondered who they were. What story did they have to tell? What struggles did they face in their lifetime? What flight were they catching, and why were they going there?

A profound thought crossed my mind as I looked at each person God had made. Each of their eternal destinies hinges on one simple question: Do they believe in Jesus? Nothing else determines where they will go after they die—not their skin color, the language they speak, the places they have lived, the money they have, the clothes they wear, or even what they have done in their lifetime (good or bad).

In the words of A.W. Tozer, "What comes into our minds when we think about God is the most important thing about us."[1] This statement holds particular significance when we are grappling with grief. Our sorrow can skew our perception of God, making us question who He is.

Though we discussed having doubts and experiencing a crisis of faith in earlier chapters, I now want to hone in on God's character. This is wildly important because as your healing journey progresses, it's important to have the right view of God. Inaccurate judgments about Him will cause you not to trust Him and will inevitably delay or even halt your healing.

For example, consider the negative ramifications of believing that God is not good, does not love you, or that He somehow wanted your baby to die. Imagine thinking He is not in control and does not care about the unjust things that happen in this world (like pregnancy and infant loss). You most likely wouldn't say out loud that you believe these things, but maybe you're like me, and deep down, sometimes you struggle with *feeling* that God can't be trusted.

So in this chapter, we will turn to His Word—instead of relying on our feelings—to remind ourselves of His true nature. Though we could explore many aspects of God's character, we will focus on the following five key attributes of God that are most often clouded by grief: His goodness, sovereignty, justice, faithfulness, and immutability.

• • • HE IS GOOD • • •

The LORD is good,
a refuge in times of trouble.

Nahum 1:7

It is hard to reconcile that a good God could allow babies to die. When we witness unspeakable tragedies, both in the world and in our own lives, we wonder how God could sit on His throne and watch them unfold without intervening.

Miscarriage, stillbirth, pandemics, genocides, child abuse, murder, drunk drivers, cancer, and wars. If He is all-powerful, why doesn't He stop these horrible things?

The horrors of sin entered the world through the Fall when God's perfect Creation became corrupted. But why did God allow sin to enter the world in the first place? My curious mind wonders, Did He *have* to put the Tree of the Knowledge of Good and Evil in the Garden?

Couldn't He have thwarted the serpent from tempting Adam and Eve? If Jesus can defeat Satan—which He did on the cross— why didn't He find a way to defeat him before humans were created and save us all the trouble of living in a broken world? Since Jesus will eventually throw Satan in the Lake of Fire, my naïve brain wonders why He couldn't have done that sooner.

I won't pretend to know why God allows evil to exist. Many theologians surmise that in order to experience God's goodness, the antithesis of good must also exist. In other words, would we grasp how amazing He is if we didn't have something to compare Him to? Perhaps God allowed evil to exist to display His love and mercy. Paul alluded to this when he said, "God has bound everyone over to disobedience so that he may have mercy on them all" (Romans 11:32).

Also, by living on this broken earth and experiencing the suffering that comes along with it, we will be even more grateful for the perfection of Heaven. Could you fully appreciate a warm, sunny day if you never experienced a cold, rainy one? Having endured the pain of this earth, we will wholeheartedly bask in God's glory and savor Heaven's splendor for all of eternity.

Because God is good, He had a good reason to allow sin to enter the world. Our finite human minds may not comprehend His ways, but we need to remember that God has already triumphed over sin, evil, and death. His restoration plan is already in the works. Tear-stained eyes may blur your vision of your hope-filled future, but don't let grief blind you to Christ's coming victory!

So, what makes God good? First and foremost, there is no evil in Him. "God is light; in him there is no darkness at all" (1 John 1:5). He will always do what is right and cannot contradict His good nature (2 Timothy 2:13). Second, from His goodness flow many of His other attributes, such as His holiness, righteousness, justice, mercy, and love.

Sweet friend, I pray you can rest in God's goodness. Instead of questioning Him, trust in His good character. God sees you and cares for you. He loves you more than you can imagine, and He has demonstrated that love for you on the cross. God is for you, not against you. Run and fall at His feet so He can comfort you. Let Him hold you, for He is good.

Faith Declaration: God is good all the time. He is good even when my baby has died. I can rely on Him to carry me through my grief.

Supporting Scripture: Psalms 34:8; 145:9; 1 Chronicles 16:34

• • • HE IS SOVEREIGN • • •

The LORD has established his throne in heaven,
and his kingdom rules over all.

Psalm 103:19

God's sovereignty is a comforting truth. He has supreme power and authority over all His Creation. He is omnipotent (all-powerful), omniscient (all-knowing), and omnipresent (existing everywhere all at once). He has infinite wisdom and knowledge. Nothing is outside of His control.

Earlier, I questioned why God allowed sin to enter the world. But we can trace it back a step further: Why did God let Lucifer fall from Heaven to begin with? This leads us to an even more profound theological question concerning God's sovereignty: Why did He create angels and humans who can reject Him?

Many scholars believe it is because God wanted His created beings to have *free will*: the *choice* to love Him. He didn't want to make robots who were forced to worship Him. Love is felt best when it is freely given. To allow angels and humans to truly love Him, He had to give them the choice to reject Him.

Some Christian camps believe God predestines all humans to Heaven or Hell without a choice. I disagree with the theological belief of "limited atonement" (that God only wants to save some humans). The Bible makes it clear that Jesus died for the sins of *all* mankind, and *whoever* should believe in Him will inherit eternal life (John 11:26). God is patient, "not wanting anyone to perish, but everyone to come to repentance" (2 Peter 3:9).

Some who believe in predestination argue that free will opposes God's sovereignty and elevates man over God. They presume that if man has the power to choose God, then he must be more powerful than Him. However, Scripture makes it clear that God can be sovereign *and* man can choose to accept His gift of salvation—at the same time.

Just because we can choose Him doesn't mean we are the ones saving ourselves. Undoubtedly, it is God's grace that saves us (through Jesus' finished work on the cross). But it requires our faith: "For it is *by grace* you have been saved, *through faith*—and this is not from yourselves, it is the gift of God—not by works so that no one can boast" (Ephesians 2:8–9, emphasis added).

Verses on predestination do not contradict humans' ability to have free will. Because God is all-knowing, He knew before the creation of the world who would end up choosing Him, a concept called *foreknowledge*. Paul told the Romans, "For those whom he foreknew he also predestined to be conformed to the image of his son" (Romans 8:29 ESV).

I will not claim to understand this mystery entirely. God's thoughts and ways are so much higher than ours (Isaiah 55:8–9). His sovereignty is complex and hard to grasp with our finite human minds. I believe it will all make sense when we get to Heaven.

When we see Jesus for the first time in Paradise, I don't think we will spend our time with Him demanding answers and complaining about our past suffering. No, we will fall face down at the sight of His glory. All we will want to do is rejoice and worship Him!

But right now, I understand that trusting in God's sovereignty comes with some really hard implications, particularly around the fact that God numbers our days. I'll be honest and say that I'm *really* struggling with this aspect of His sovereignty in my current season of grief.

My dad was only sixty-four years old when a drunk driver killed him. He was healthy and had his retirement and golden years ahead of him. In my mind, he had at least another twenty good years left to live. In those twenty years, I imagined we would have spent a lot of time together, taken many family trips, and made many more memories.

So, why did God number my dad's days like that? Why did he have to die so young and in such a tragic way? I do not know! I may never fully understand why on this side of Heaven. I wonder the same about why God allows babies to die before they even get to take a single breath or make a single memory on earth.

Why did God only let Bridget live for twenty-four weeks and five days in my womb? Why did He let *your* baby die when they did? Oh, friend, these are hard but honest and healthy questions, and you are not alone in asking them! But here's where I've had to land my restless thoughts—which, if I dig down deep, stem from my persistent need to understand and control all things. I am not the Author of Life (Acts 3:15), and I do not hold the authority to number a person's days (Job 14:5). God numbered the days of Bridget's life and knew she would live 173 days inside my womb. Her days were ordained and written in God's book before one of them came to be (Psalm 139:16).

Does this mean His purpose was for her to be stillborn, or that He just allowed it? I can't say for sure. Though this uncertainty may make us uncomfortable (and may bring us back to the never-ending loop of *why* questions), it brings me peace to know Bridget fulfilled her life as He intended.

However, my grieving heart has the tendency to wallow in the should-have-beens, such as "She should have been ten years old this year." Do you do the same? Though it's natural to think this way, I must remind myself that Bridget has already lived the life God meant for her to live. It was never the plan for her to be a ten-year-old on this earth. Because she is already in Heaven, this hypothetical situation is outside of reality and His will.

I understand how painful it can be to hear such a statement. I cringe at it too. But if we wholly trust in His sovereignty, we can surrender the "could-have-been" for the "what-is-now." Instead of imagining our children at the age they "should be" now, we can have peace knowing that our child is alive in Heaven and that we will see them again one day.

Also, God sees the bigger picture when He numbers our days and our babies' days. He made us eternal beings whose lives have no end. From an earthly perspective, we might think some lives are being cut short, but from a Heavenly perspective, those lives are simply being ushered into His glorious Kingdom sooner!

Imagine a piece of infinite string representing our lives—green representing our time on earth and white representing our time in Heaven. Some people would have more green on their string than others. Yet, all of our string lengths would be the same (never-ending).

When we look at the string analogy from our vantage point on earth, we feel sad for the people with a shorter green span of string. But if we looked down from Heaven, in its perfect splendor, wouldn't we feel sad for the people who had to endure this broken world longer? We would envy people who had more white on their strings. It's all dependent on our perspective!

Because God sees all of eternity, we should trust in His sovereignty and His plan for both our lives and our babies' lives. The number of their days on earth has no bearing on their eternal dwelling! He is holding them in His good and loving arms until we get there.

> **Faith Declaration**: God is on His throne. He is in control. He is sovereign over my life and my baby's life. We will live together forever.
>
> **Supporting Scripture**: 1 Chronicles 29:11–12; Job 42:2; Proverbs 16:9; Romans 8:28

• • • HE IS JUST • • •

He is the Rock, his works are perfect,
and all his ways are just.
A faithful God who does no wrong,
upright and just is he.

Deuteronomy 32:4

Do you feel that life is unfair? It certainly doesn't feel fair that death has separated you from your child. We live in a world where a million injustices happen every single second. Nothing about this earth is right or fair. Sin has plagued and decayed everything: the earth, our bodies, relationships, and governments.

I feel righteous anger when I witness something unjust, and when it happens to *me*, I feel it even more. When we know God's Word and understand right from wrong, we *should* be broken-hearted over injustices that grieve God's heart. Jesus Himself modeled righteous indignation for us. He overturned tables at the temple when He saw people using His house of worship as a place to exploit people financially (Matthew 21:12).

The desire for justice is ingrained in us because we were made in the image of the greatest Judge. He wired us this way because justice is an innate attribute of His character. However, because we are sinful, our justice system is broken. We are unable to execute true justice. Thankfully, God's laws are perfect. He is impartial and does not take bribes (Deuteronomy 10:17). "God does not show favoritism" (Romans 2:11).

His justice and righteousness are the foundation of His throne (Psalm 89:14), and He will judge the world with righteousness (Psalm 98:9). We can rejoice over this fact. Even though things are unfair right now, one day, He will right every wrong and redeem all that sin has stolen. The best part? His redemption plan is already underway!

Jesus already made His sacrifice on the cross to restore humanity to Himself. At the coming Resurrection of the dead, we will trade our broken mortal bodies for glorified immortal ones. All will be made new! We will live forever with our children and loved ones in Christ on the New Earth. In His ultimate justice, God has reserved this sin-stained earth for fire (2 Peter 3:10).

The King James translation says the earth will melt with "fervent heat," and the works in it will be burned up. How's that for justice? Knowing He has a plan to make all things right, we can trust Him when we grieve over the brokenness of this world. Redemption is coming (Luke 21:28), and we must hold on a little longer.

> **Faith Declaration:** God is just. He will make all things right. God will wipe away all my tears. He will reunite me with my baby.
>
> **Supporting Scripture:** Psalms 11:7; 33:4–5; Isaiah 5:16; 9:7; 30:18

• • • HE IS FAITHFUL • • •

Let us hold fast the confession of our hope without wavering, for he who promised is faithful.

Hebrews 10:23 ESV

God is faithful. This one feels the most intimate and personal of all His attributes. When you think of what characteristics you most desire in a friend or spouse, loyalty and reliability are probably at the top of your list. Our hearts desire someone who will stick with us through thick and thin and love us unconditionally.

God uses a marriage metaphor throughout the Bible to describe the relationship between Christ and the Church. Paul explained to the Ephesians that in the same way the husband is the head of his wife, Jesus is the head of His body, the Church (5:23). He refers to the Church as the Bride of Christ.

When brides and grooms stand at the altar and say their marriage vows, they promise to be faithful to each other until "death do us part." Fidelity is the foundation of a marriage covenant. Without it, everything in the relationship falls apart: trust, communication, intimacy, respect, and love.

Some of you have been hurt, as I have been, by someone you loved and trusted—perhaps an ex-boyfriend, spouse, family member, or friend. The sting of rejection or betrayal by a man, especially if by a father or husband, can negatively impact your view of God as a faithful and loving Father.

But unlike humans who can go back on their word and disappoint us, God will never break His vows to us. He has committed Himself to us for eternity. He will never leave or forsake us. Oh, what love is this! It is the unconditional love our hearts so desire.

The Bible describes different types of love, depending on the word used in the original language. The Greek word *agape* is used over one hundred times in the New Testament. Agape love is based on choice and commitment, not emotion or feelings. It is the "highest, most pure form of love."[2]

Jesus expressed this kind of sacrificial love by dying on the cross for us. John affirmed that Jesus embodies agape love when he stated, "Greater love has no one than this: to lay down one's life for one's friends" (John 15:13). Jesus loves you so much that He died for you.

He will be your faithful friend and ever-present help in times of trouble (Psalm 46:1). As you grieve your baby, He will not leave your side. David wrote that God hems us in (Psalm 139:5). He goes before us and behind us. What beautiful imagery that He is all around us, encircling us in His faithful love.

> **Faith Declaration**: God is faithful. He loves me and will never leave me. God is loyal to His Word. He will not break His promises to me.
>
> **Supporting Scripture**: Psalm 33:4; 2 Thessalonians 3:3; 1 Corinthians 1:9

• • • HE IS IMMUTABLE • • •

Jesus Christ is the same yesterday and today and forever.

Hebrews 13:8

Lastly, God is immutable: He never changes. He is *always* the same. Our circumstances and perspectives of Him cannot change Him. Because He never changes, none of His attributes ever change: God is good all the time, sovereign all the time, just all the time, and faithful all the time.

So often, we let our perpetually revolving circumstances distort who we believe God is. But who are we to think that God is who He is based on what's going on in *our lives*? There are billions of people on this earth; God would constantly change every second if He were tied to each person's life circumstances. God *can't* be this way. He is who He is, and He never changes.

This is good news for us! We wouldn't want His character to depend on the shaky ground of our human experience. God's love for us never changes. We can't earn more love from Him than we already have. We don't have to muster up good works to attain His favor. He loves us the same in the valley and on the mountaintop. No earthly experience, grief, or loss can shake His great love for us. You are truly the apple of His eye (Psalm 17:8; Zechariah 2:8).

Paul declared, "Neither height nor depth, nor anything else in all creation, will be able to separate us from the love of God that is in Christ Jesus our Lord" (Romans 8:39). He loved us so much that while we were still sinners, He died for us (Romans 5:8). His agape love is consistent and never-changing. No matter where you are in your grief journey, He is the same today, tomorrow, and always.

> **Faith Declaration:** God never changes. He will always be the same. I can always trust Him.
>
> **Supporting Scripture:** James 1:17; Numbers 23:19; 1 Samuel 15:29

PRAYERS TO HEAVEN

God, we are so glad You are a good God whose character never changes. We can trust in Your sovereignty even when our life has fallen apart. Thank You for being faithful to us even when we don't deserve it. You are a God who keeps Your promises. Help us to remember that You are a loving Father who will never leave us. You are holding our broken hearts close to Yours. We need You like we need breath in our lungs. Thank You for

Your justice and plan to make all things right. We love You and praise You for who You are! Amen.

TRUTH TO CLING TO

Psalm 25:8 (Good); Proverbs 19:21 (Sovereign); Job 34:12; 2 Chronicles 19:7; Ecclesiastes 3:17 (Just); Lamentations 3:22–23 (Faithful); Malachi 3:6 (Immutable)

TIME WITH JESUS

1. A.W. Tozer wrote that what you think about God is the most important thing about you. Write down your honest thoughts on how you view God right now.
2. Which of the five attributes of God's character is hardest for you to believe? Why?
3. Which of the five attributes of God's character gives you the most hope and comfort? Why?

HEALING STEPS

1. Read the Supporting Scripture from the attribute you find hardest to believe. Write your favorite one on a sticky note and post it on your bathroom mirror.
2. Memorize the Faith Declaration from the attribute you find hardest to believe. Repeat it out loud daily.
3. Listen to the hymn "Great Is Thy Faithfulness" and reflect on God's never-changing character.

7

Grace upon Grace

WHEN YOU CAN'T FORGIVE YOURSELF

There is therefore now no condemnation for those who are in
Christ Jesus.

Romans 8:1

Trigger Warning: medical trauma

Flashback to Bridget's birth // I woke up and knew something was
different about this morning. An intense stabbing pain gripped
my lower abdomen. I called my mom, a postpartum nurse, and
asked her to come over.

Matt had gone to work, and I didn't want to be alone. The
week before, I had been hospitalized due to increased bleeding.
After being monitored, they determined I wasn't in labor and
sent me home. So I wasn't sure if this was another scare or the
real thing. By the time my mom arrived, I knew I needed to be
taken to the hospital right away.

My water suddenly broke, and I became nauseous. I grabbed the towel bar in the bathroom with clammy hands and tried to stabilize myself. *This is it. It's happening now.* My mom helped me into the passenger seat of my SUV. She called Matt, who left work immediately to meet us at the hospital.

I will never forget that drive. The pain I felt. The thoughts I had. *Is my daughter alive? If she is, will she be strong enough to survive birth?* She was only twenty-four weeks and five days' gestation, and she measured three to four weeks behind on growth scans. The hemorrhage was preventing my placenta from nourishing her and allowing her to grow fully. I felt helpless and panicked at my inability to save her.

Fears swirled in my mind as the excruciating physical pain fought to demand all of my attention. We pulled up to the emergency room, and a nurse guided me into a wheelchair and quickly pushed me to the labor and delivery unit.

Nurses lifted me into the bed and removed my clothes, cloaking me in a muted green hospital gown. I writhed in pain as they poked and prodded both arms, hands, and wrists to get the IV into my small veins. I requested an epidural to alleviate the pain, but they told me there wasn't enough time. I was fully dilated, and they expected my baby to be born very soon.

Matt arrived and held my hand as a nurse wrapped monitoring belts around my small bump of a belly. We waited anxiously to hear her heartbeat, a sound we had heard many times before on our home Doppler. *Ba-boom, ba-boom,* always around 160 beats per minute, like little galloping horses—but the equipment was eerily quiet this time.

One of the nurses commented that she possibly heard a faint heartbeat. That was the last thing I remember before I felt an incredible pressure to push and then a release from my intense physical pain.

"She's here," my mom proclaimed as a nurse delivered my daughter and quickly assessed her for signs of life. What followed was silence. No cries, no gasps for air. I don't remember what was said to declare that Bridget was already in Heaven, but somehow, I knew.

I lay in a daze as my OB stood between my legs, blocking my view of my daughter. She then delivered my placenta and afterward pulled out the massive hemorrhage clot that had been behind it. She placed both in a bedpan and leaned them over to show me that the clot was *larger* than the placenta.

My OB declared, "This clot saved your life. Without it, you would have bled to death." I was shocked at the insensitivity of her words, though she was simply stating a medical fact. I didn't care about *my* life! This clot was the culprit that killed my baby! How would I ever forgive my body for doing this to my sweet girl?

◦ ◦ ◦ ALREADY BUT NOT YET ◦ ◦ ◦

For months after Bridget was born, I wouldn't look at my body when undressing for the shower. Feelings of failure and shame flooded my heart every time I glanced at my naked frame. I looked away, hating my body for what it did to her. I had trusted my body to protect, nurture, and grow her, but it failed me—and even worse, it failed her. Maybe you feel this way too?

The good news is that God didn't create our bodies to fail us (and they won't stay this way forever). When He made man and woman in the Garden on the sixth day, He saw that everything He had made "was very good" (Genesis 1:31 KJV). However, after the Fall, God said to Eve: "I will make your pains in childbearing very severe; with painful labor you will give birth to children" (Genesis 3:16).

Painful labor was a consequence of the Fall, but the main result of Adam and Eve's sin was—and continues to be—death. Thankfully, Jesus came to earth and purchased our salvation with His blood, saving us from death and promising us eternal life.

However, we live in the *already but not yet*: *after* the cross but *before* the Resurrection. We are already redeemed but not yet resurrected. Our bodies are still broken, awaiting our glorified ones.

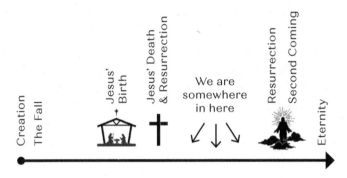

*Shows the general order of events; not to time scale

At the trumpet call, Jesus will raise us to life in our glorified, resurrected bodies—ones not subject to illness, injury, or death. We will be caught up in the air with Him, "and so we will be with the Lord forever" (1 Thessalonians 4:17). Praise God for this blessed hope (Titus 2:13)!

But what do you do now, when the death of your baby has caused you to harbor anger and bitterness toward your body? What happens when the lines blur between body and self, and you begin to resent not just your body, but *yourself*?

• • • YOU ARE A GOOD MOM • • •

Somehow, we wrongly assume that if our body couldn't sustain life, then we must not be good enough to be a mother. We accept the lie that our miscarriage or stillbirth reflects something about our motherhood. So instead of feeling as if *your body* failed your baby, you feel as though *you* failed your baby.

This is a lie from the enemy. I know that if there was something you could have done to save your baby, you would have. You did not cause your baby to die. And most likely, you could not have prevented it either. You did everything within your power to keep your baby safe. You are a good mom!

Can you give yourself grace for not knowing what you didn't know? Can you recognize there were things outside of your control that you couldn't change? Do you see that the things you know now are because you went through what you went through? You couldn't possibly have had that same knowledge prior to your experience.

After Bridget passed away, I went to several doctors searching for medical answers for her death. I knew I had a subchorionic hemorrhage and placental abruption in her pregnancy, but why? Would this happen again? Could I do something differently to prevent this from happening to another baby?

In my quest for answers, doctors diagnosed me with a thyroid disorder and confirmed that my polycystic ovary syndrome was causing issues related to low progesterone. Although I struggled with infertility for several years, God ultimately blessed me with two precious boys, Bridget's little brothers. During my pregnancies with them, I was on thyroid medication and progesterone suppositories and injections.

After delivering both of them full-term and healthy, I wondered if Bridget would have lived if I had been on progesterone with her. But whenever I think this way, I remind myself there was no reason for me to believe I needed progesterone at the time. Why would a mom with no history of loss take progesterone in her first pregnancy? She wouldn't. *I didn't know what I didn't know.*

It was only because of Bridget that I discovered this root hormonal problem. Though her life had many purposes, I believe one was preparing my body for her brothers' healthy pregnancies. In a way, her life saved theirs. But some of you will never know why your baby died.

Though you have gone to the appointments, taken the lab tests, and done the sonograms, doctors have left you with no answers and an apprehension about the future. I understand how debilitating this can be. It's hard to move forward without answers, but I pray you will surrender the unknown to God and trust that He has a good plan for your future (whether that involves trying for more children or not).

It wasn't until two years after Bridget went to Heaven that we started trying to grow our family. I needed time to grieve her, and I was also busy starting the ministry. I knew my body needed time to recover physically, but I also wasn't ready emotionally or spiritually. After all the trauma I had gone through in my pregnancy with Bridget, I was scared of getting pregnant again.

I couldn't imagine losing another child. I reflected on what I once heard a pastor say: What you fear the most is where you trust God the least. I realized I trusted God the least with my children because my greatest fear was losing them. I needed to surrender control to God and trust Him with my children's lives— Bridget's *and* those of any future children we would have. So we decided to wait to start trying until our faith was greater than our fear.

• • • Forgiving Yourself for Decisions • • • You Made

Maybe you don't struggle with body resentment, but perhaps you look back on your baby's short life in your womb and have regrets. You wish you had enjoyed your pregnancy more—cherishing each kick and talking to your baby—but you felt so nauseous and tired that there were times you wished you weren't even pregnant. Now that you've lost your baby, you feel guilt and shame. You wonder if God punished you for not being more excited or happy about being pregnant.

Maybe there's a moment in your pregnancy that keeps haunting you. The day you noticed decreased movement but didn't go to the hospital right away. It could be the food you ate, the medicine you took, the sickness you had, the long car ride you went on, or the strenuous activity you did. When you think of it, your heart sinks to your stomach: Did I cause this? Could I have done something to prevent it?

Maybe you beat yourself up over decisions you made—or didn't make—at the time of your baby's birth. Perhaps you chose not to have family members or siblings come and hold your baby, and now you wish you had. Or maybe you turned down the offer to have professional photography taken of your stillborn baby. It felt too hard at the time, but now you would do anything to have pictures of your sweet baby's face.

Although we had Now I Lay Me Down to Sleep (NILMDTS) remembrance photographs taken of Bridget, I didn't think to capture her on video. I wish we had videos of us holding her, but it did not cross our minds. What about you? What regrets do you have? What has helped me with these regrets is to give myself the same grace I would give someone else in the same position. What would I tell a friend who confided in me that she felt sad over not having videos of her stillborn baby?

I would say, "I'm so sorry you don't have videos of your baby. I can see how devastating that would be. But give yourself grace. You had just lost a baby. You were in shock and going through your worst nightmare. In the midst of the trauma and heartbreak, why would you have thought to take videos? It's not your fault." Wouldn't you say something similar?

Another common regret I frequently hear from grieving moms surrounds the topic of their baby's final resting place. Maybe you chose communal burial or hospital disposition, and now you wish you had done a private burial or cremation. First, let me assure you that their resting place is temporary—one day, no matter where they are, Jesus will resurrect their body. Take comfort in knowing your choice has no bearing on their eternal state.

But it's still painful to wish you had made different decisions. The playback loop we run in our minds of all the what-ifs and could-have-beens can be agonizing. The enemy wants to keep us focused on the past and living in a perpetual state of shame and self-blame. We need to get our minds out of this loop to accept what has happened—as awful and painful as it was—and move forward focused on the hope-filled future God has for us.

Acceptance doesn't mean we like what happened, but it keeps us from getting stuck in the trauma of the past. Remember, there is now no condemnation in Christ (Romans 8:1). By His mercy, we can extend grace to our bodies—and to ourselves—even if we still carry the weight of self-blame, despite knowing we could not have prevented our baby's death. In doing so, we will rightly see our bodies for what they are: a temple of the Most High God.

• • • YOUR BODY IS A TEMPLE • • •

Did you know God calls your body sacred? Paul wrote, "Don't you know that *you yourselves are God's temple* and that God's Spirit dwells in your midst? If anyone destroys God's temple, God will destroy that person; for God's temple is *sacred*" (1 Corinthians 3:16–17, emphasis added).

Paul further elaborated: "Do you not know that your body is a temple of the Holy Spirit within you" (6:19 ESV)? He does not call our bodies sacred because we have the perfect physique. Nor does our sacredness depend on whether our wombs delivered healthy, living babies. Our bodies are sacred *because He dwells within us*!

Humans are divinely distinct from all the other creatures God created. This uniqueness stems from being made in His image. God Himself is tripartite (made of three parts), consisting of the Father, Son, and Holy Spirit. Similarly, we are tripartite—consisting of a body, soul, and spirit.

Paul affirmed this distinction: "May your whole *spirit, soul, and body* be kept blameless at the coming of our Lord Jesus Christ" (1 Thessalonians 5:23, emphasis added). I have outlined the differences between these three parts in the chart below.

Part	Greek Word	Dimension	Consciousness	Description
Body	*Sōma*	Physical	World-Consciousness	Your visible, outer part; how you experience the material world; your five senses
Soul	*Psychē*	Psychological	Self-Consciousness	Your sense of self; your personality; how you think, reason, and feel
Spirit	*Pneuma*	Spiritual	God-Consciousness	Your innermost, eternal being; your connection to God; where His Spirit dwells in you

What sets us apart from animals, birds, and fish is the presence of a spirit, made in His image (Genesis 1:26–27; 2:7; Zechariah 12:1). Jesus proclaimed, "No one can enter the kingdom of God unless they are born of water and the Spirit. Flesh gives birth to flesh, but the Spirit gives birth to spirit" (John 3:5–6).

When we surrender our lives to Jesus, His Holy Spirit dwells within our spirit, forming a direct connection to Him. John the apostle wrote, "God is spirit, and his worshipers must worship in the Spirit and in truth" (John 4:24). However, since we live in a physical world, our spirits need physical dwellings. Our bodies serve as the earthly vessels that contain our souls, which house our spirits.

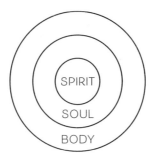

God also designed women to grow life *inside* their bodies in an intimate place called the womb. During pregnancy, there is quite literally another soul inside your body. This is such a sacred place; it is no wonder that the death of a baby would have such a profound impact on a woman's soul.

• • • Knit Together • • •

Why did translators use the English word *knit* to describe God's process of creating human life in a mother's womb? In Psalm 139:13, David proclaims, "For you created my inmost being; you knit me together in my mother's womb."

In the first part of this verse, "my inmost being" is translated from the Hebrew word *kilyah*, which means kidneys or innermost parts (such as the heart, organs, and veins). Think of how complex God's design of the human body is, with each cell, bone, tendon, muscle, and artery having a specific purpose.

However, *kelayot* (plural for kidneys) is sometimes figuratively used to refer to a person's reins—meaning their mind or feelings. For example, let's read from Jeremiah 11:20: "But, O Lord of hosts, that judgest righteously, that triest the reins and the heart" (KJV). "Triest the reins" comes from the Hebrew *bochen kelayot*—meaning that God judges our emotions and affections.

The verb *knit* (used in various translations, such as the NIV and ESV) comes from the Hebrew word *sakhakh* and refers to the interweaving and entwining God does as He creates a human being. The King James Version translates this as "covered" from the Hebrew verb *cake*,[1] which means to cover or protect. God gives us a physical body to protect our innermost parts (our spirit and soul).

This intimate language in Psalm 139 continues in verse 15: "My frame was not hidden from you, when I was made in the secret place. When I was woven together in the depths of the earth."

"Woven together" comes from the Hebrew word *raqam*, which the King James Version translates as "curiously wrought."

In both cases, we see an intentional act of stitching and weaving—not only of our physical parts but of our three parts: body, spirit, and soul. Yes, God intricately wove our babies' genes, cells, organs, and tissues to form their bodies inside our wombs. But something even more extraordinary happened inside us: God created our babies' eternal spirits and wove them inside *their* bodies *inside us.*

Conception is not merely the miraculous union of a mother's and father's DNA but a profound moment when God breathes life into a human's spirit and soul. Paul affirmed that we are made up of more than just a body when he stated, "If there is a natural body, there is also a spiritual body" (1 Corinthians 15:44). And it is this spiritual part of us—and our babies—that never dies.

I once heard a mother who had suffered recurrent miscarriages refer to her womb as a graveyard, the place where her babies died. From an earthly perspective, it may seem that our bodies gave birth to death, but from a Heavenly perspective—*because of Jesus*—our bodies gave birth to eternal life.

We can view our bodies in two ways: the place where our baby *died* or the place where they *lived* before going Home. I don't know what it's like for a soul to travel from earth to Heaven, but the idea that Bridget's soul left *her* body inside *my* body brings me great comfort.

Initially, the thought of her dying inside of me used to bother me. I agonized over what it must have been like for her: Did she suffer or feel pain? Was she scared? When, exactly, did she die? Are you also troubled by these disturbing thoughts? Have you ever wondered where you were and what you were doing when your baby's heart stopped beating?

You are not alone in despairing over these details. However, I have learned to entrust them to the Lord, knowing that any pain Bridget *may* have endured was momentary and insignificant compared with the eternal joy she is now experiencing in Heaven. She is not suffering anymore. That moment is long over for her; it continues only in my mind. Bridget left the warmth of my womb for the wonder of Paradise.

At her gestational age, she could hear my heartbeat and maybe even my voice. All she ever knew was my love. Her short life was not wasted. God's knitting wasn't incomplete! Though she weighed only thirteen ounces at delivery, God had already knit her soul and secured her spirit for eternity.

I agree with the famous Tennyson lines, "'Tis better to have loved and lost / Than never to have loved at all."[2] I would endure the pregnancy complications and eleven weeks on bed rest again to hold Bridget for another twenty-four hours. I would suffer the pain and shed the tears all over again to see her for just one more day. Because if God hadn't given me those twenty-four weeks and five days with her, I wouldn't have a daughter for all of eternity.

I imagine most of us would rather have loved and lost our baby than never to have had them at all. The suffering was worth the love! For followers of Christ, the time spent growing our babies in our wombs—no matter how brief—has afforded us an *eternity* in Heaven with them. We haven't "lost" them at all. We know where they are, and we will one day be with them again.

I penned these words in my prayer journal two days after Bridget's birth: "Waking up no longer pregnant this morning was so hard. I feel so much guilt that I failed Bridget as a mother. I hate my body for not doing what it was supposed to do. But then I see that God used it to create her, and I have a hard time hating it so much."

Momma, in collaboration with the Creator, your body housed and grew your precious baby. Can you forgive your body and see it as the beautiful blessing that it is? Though your body is currently broken, God gifted you a child through it—one you will run, dance, and play with forever in your glorified bodies.

PRAYERS TO HEAVEN

Jesus, thank You for creating us in Your image and forming our innermost being. Our souls ache that our bodies failed at sustaining our baby's life. We struggle with blaming ourselves for their death. Give us grace upon grace to forgive ourselves. Remind us that our bodies are sacred temples and that through them, You blessed us with the gift of our children. Thank You for knitting them in our wombs. We are humbled to be their mothers. We praise You for the coming Resurrection and the hope we have to spend eternity with our babies in glorified bodies. Amen.

TRUTH TO CLING TO

Genesis 2:7 KJV; Zechariah 12:1; John 1:16–17; Romans 5:20–21; 2 Corinthians 12:9–10; Titus 2:11–14; Hebrews 4:15–16

TIME WITH JESUS

1. Do you blame your body for your baby's death? Ask Jesus to help you forgive your body and see it for what it is: a sacred temple that houses His Spirit and grew your precious baby. Write a prayer of gratitude for your body and the blessing of your baby.

2. As you reflect on your pregnancy and baby's birth, the what-ifs and could-have-beens can be debilitating. Surrender your anxious thoughts and regrets to the Lord. Ask Him to cover you in His grace and free you from shame and self-blame.

3. Read Psalm 139 and reflect on how we are made of three parts: body, soul, and spirit. Fill out the diagram in your *CIH Guided Journal.*

HEALING STEPS

1. You are a good mom. You didn't cause your baby to die. Write a letter of forgiveness to yourself. Offer yourself the same grace and compassion you would show a friend. At the bottom of your letter, write out Romans 8:1.

2. The next time you get in the shower, look at your body. Instead of seeing your body as a place of death, see it as the place your baby lived. Thank God for choosing you to be your baby's mother.

3. Fill in the blanks below or in your *CIH Guided Journal.* Place it somewhere you will see it daily.

Thank you, Jesus, for choosing me, _____, to be _____'s mother. I am grateful You knit _____ in my womb. I praise You for making _____ with an eternal spirit that lives with You in Heaven. I can't wait for the Resurrection when we will receive our glorified bodies and live together forever! As I wait for that day, hold _____ and tell them how much I love them.

8

They Know Not
What They Do

WHEN YOU ARE HURT BY OTHERS

And when they came to the place that is called The Skull, there
they crucified him, and the criminals, one on his right and one
on his left. And Jesus said, "Father, forgive them, for they know
not what they do."

Luke 23:33–34 ESV

Trigger Warning: living children

I shuffled through the pea gravel surrounding the playground.
I repositioned myself to keep a close eye on my three-year-old
son, who was dashing between scaling ladders, tottering across
a wobbly bridge, and whizzing down the "big boy" slides.

As he stood at the top of the play structure, I walked over to
an opening to talk to him as two little kids, a brother and sister,

passed him on their way to the slide. As the boy noticed my son playing alone, he blurted to his mom, "Oh, he doesn't have a sister like me." His mom, standing nearby, responded, "Yeah, he doesn't have a sister."

When her words reached my ears, they cut straight to my heart and reverberated in its broken chambers. *He. Doesn't. Have. A. Sister.* Five simple words held the power to resurface all my grief for Bridget and derail my entire day. I thought, *How dare she say that?*

In my triggered emotional state, I didn't have the courage to correct her out loud. Instead, I responded in my head: *He does have a sister. You just can't see her because she is in Heaven.* Tears welled up in my eyes, and I felt the need to leave. I quietly took hold of my son's hand and walked somberly to my car. The rest of the day, I ruminated over those five words and how sad I was that my son didn't have his sister to play with him.

Have you experienced something similar? Whether it was a stranger, a family member, a friend, or a coworker, have someone's words caused your emotions to tailspin? In my years of ministry, I have facilitated dozens of support groups, and the topic of hurtful words is a common thread in almost every one. It's disheartening, but not surprising, that every bereaved mom I've met has been hurt by someone in her grief.

Words, as we know, hold tremendous power. They can either hurt or heal you, strengthen or destroy you. "The tongue has the power of life and death" (Proverbs 18:21). Our hearts are more sensitive in grief, giving words even more power to build us up or tear us down.

• • • A TALE OF TWO CUPS • • •

I want you to imagine two cups sitting on a counter. The first cup is mostly full of water, with an inch of room at the top. The second cup is full to the brim. Now picture adding a drop of water to each cup. The water droplet will cause a small ripple in the first cup but barely disturb its contents.

But the drop added to the second cup will cause the water to overflow, resulting in a mess on the counter. Each subsequent drop, no matter how small, will continue the spillage. A psychiatrist used this analogy to explain to me how trauma and pain can cause our lives to be emotionally "at the brim." Any subsequent disruption in our lives results in magnified reactions and spilling over of pent-up emotions.

When life is steady and normal, our emotions are like the first cup. Minor disturbances and inconveniences do not disrupt our peace or warrant a significant response. However, when grief enters our world, sadness and anxiety fill our cups to the brim like the second cup. The most minor occurrences—a hurtful word, a snippy remark, a slight setback in our day—can cause our emotions to pour over.

This analogy helped me understand why small situations often caused me to react with big emotions, like when that mom at the park commented about my son's apparent lack of a sister. Though the interaction didn't elicit an outwardly emotional response, at least not one noticeable to her or anyone else at the park, the damage was done internally. I let her words have power over my emotional state, which ruined the time I was supposed to be enjoying with my son.

• • • THE GRACE CUP • • •

While I am on the train of using cup analogies, I want to share another that has transformed my ability to navigate life after loss: the Grace Cup. It starts with this basic premise: Most of the time, with a few exceptions, people do not intend to hurt us with their words.

The mom at the park had no idea I had lost a daughter. She was simply making an observation based on what her eyes could see. She did not intend to hurt me. What if I had offered her grace instead of getting upset and feeling offended? Well, it would have protected *my* peace. Instead of taking her comment to heart, I could have taken it to God and then enjoyed the rest of my time with my son.

Because these occurrences often happen when we least expect them, we should prefill our Grace Cup and be ready to pour it on people in everyday situations. Instead of walking around unsure of when we will step on the next land mine, we should expect someone to say something insensitive at some point.

This means we *predetermine* that our response in these situations will be grace. When someone refers to my oldest son as my firstborn? Grace. When someone calls me a boy mom? Grace. When someone says I have two children? Grace. The Grace Cup is a symbolic tool we use to protect our emotional well-being in the face of hurtful words.

Now, you may be thinking, *Grace. They don't deserve it! Why do I have to be the one offering grace when I'm grieving my baby, and they're the ones saying hurtful things?* I understand your feelings, and they are valid. But offering grace is not about them; it's about you.

You do not want to live in a state of constant hurt and offense! A victimhood mentality will lend itself to a lifetime of resentment, bitterness, and anger. When we deny others our forgiveness, we give them power over us. Holding on to unforgiveness will hurt you more than anyone else.

As hard as it may be to hear this, God does not give us a pass to withhold forgiveness because we've lost a child. Our grief doesn't give us the right to hold others' insensitive words and actions over their heads. As followers of Jesus, He calls us to forgive others, regardless of our circumstances. Paul said we should forgive others because Jesus has forgiven us *first*:

- "Forgive one another if any of you has a grievance against someone. Forgive as the Lord forgave you" (Colossians 3:13).

- "Be kind to one another, tenderhearted, forgiving one another, as God in Christ forgave you" (Ephesians 4:32 ESV).

Offering forgiveness isn't based on whether a person deserves it. Even if someone purposely said something hurtful and never repented or apologized, Jesus asks us to forgive them. He died for us while we were still sinners and undeserving of His mercy. Who are we, who were shown such lavish grace, to withhold it from others?

Forgiveness means granting unmerited grace to those who hurt you, but it doesn't mean forgetting what someone said or did. Their hurtful words or actions may still cause you pain. It is possible to forgive without forgetting. Instead of dwelling on what they did, you can choose to focus on (1) how God will sanctify you through the suffering they have caused and (2) how He will grow your testimony to reach others for His glory.

As hard as it is to do, we should forgive others just as Jesus forgave the Roman soldiers who crucified Him. Hanging on the cross, He cried out, "Father, forgive them, for they know not what they do" (Luke 23:34 ESV). In the same way, those who hurt you "know not what they do." My sweet friend, hold out your Grace Cup, which has been prefilled with the grace of Jesus, and stand ready to pour it out.

• • • GOOD INTENTIONS • • •

Most hurtful words toward grieving moms are unintentional. They usually fall into two categories:

1. Someone felt uncomfortable and didn't know what to say, so they accidentally said something insensitive. Even worse, sometimes they say nothing at all.
2. Someone felt bad for us and tried to say something helpful, but it came across as hurtful instead.

We've all heard the platitudes or religious clichés people offer to make us feel better. Though well-intended, their statements attempt to justify our loss and inadvertently minimize our grief. Most people's intentions are good at their core. They want to comfort us because they love us. It's hard for them to see us in pain, so they try to fix it so that they can see us happy again.

People are uncomfortable discussing death, especially that of a baby. Ironically enough, when they try to avoid saying the wrong thing, they end up saying the wrong thing! They attempt to search for the silver lining in our grief and offer unsolicited advice. However, most of the time, their message is misconstrued.

Honestly, before I experienced stillbirth myself, I probably said something insensitive or didn't show up for someone in the way I should have. Experiencing loss has made me more compassionate toward others. It taught me how to empathize with people who are going through loss or difficult times.

What about you? Before your loss, would you have known how to comfort someone who was grieving? Would you have said the perfect words to a mom who just lost a baby? I know I didn't. This has taught me to have grace for those who *know not what they do*. By recognizing the intentions and heart behind their words, we can choose to see the best in people.

But please know that I do understand how difficult it is to navigate strained relationships while grieving the loss of your baby. It was a side effect I least expected after losing Bridget. I assumed people would understand the pain I was going through and support me in meaningful ways.

Unfortunately, this was not always the case. Though many people showed up for me in beautiful ways, some of my friends did not. When I went back to work, some coworkers and clients avoided the subject and did not even acknowledge that I had lost a baby. All of this caused grief on top of grief!

I hope you have family and friends who support you in the ways you need. If you do, hold on to them tightly. They are the rare friendships you want to keep for a lifetime. But if you've experienced disappointment in some of your relationships, let's discuss how to navigate them graciously while protecting your heart from hurt.

• • • COMMUNICATION IS KEY • • •

When drowning in grief, it feels unnatural and maybe even awkward to tell people you are hurting. You lost a baby. Shouldn't they just know you need their support? Yes! In an ideal world, they would see that you are heartbroken, swoop in, and love on you.

Some people do this really well, and we praise God for them. Unfortunately, others may not show up for you or support you fully because they lack the time or emotional capacity due to their own life circumstances and unhealed pain. I've learned people can only give you what they already have. Seek out people who exude the qualities you hope to attain through your grief journey.

Do you want to find joy in your sorrow? Find someone who endured hardship and came out the other side with a newfound joy in the Lord. If you desire biblical guidance and encouragement, find a believer who knows Scripture like the back of their hand. As mentioned in Proverbs 12:18, "The words of the reckless pierce like swords, but the tongue of the wise brings healing."

But what if you are hurt by your closest family and friends? Many grieving moms have tearfully recounted to me the painful exchanges of words that pierced their hearts. I nod my head in solidarity and silently acknowledge their pain. But my follow-up question usually surprises them: "Did you tell your friend or family member how they made you feel?"

Usually, the answer is no. I understand expressing your feelings to someone you love can be uncomfortable, but how will they know that they hurt you if you don't tell them? Hurt feelings and unresolved tension can lead to broken relationships. Communication is key to avoiding relational damage.

In the midst of deep grief, you might try to make it appear—on the outside—as though you're doing better than you are. Maybe you muster a smile and an "okay" when someone asks how you're doing. But really, you feel nowhere close to okay—on the inside, you are falling apart and don't know how you're going to get through the day.

Oh, sweet friend, don't be afraid or ashamed to respond to the question "How are you?" with "Not great," "I've been better," or "I'm just really sad." It can feel awkward telling others exactly how you're feeling, but I've found that being honest opens the door for others to love you better (and models to them how to grieve authentically).

People can't help you if they don't know you're hurting, and they won't know *how* to help you if you don't tell them what you need. They can't read your mind. They don't know what you need and are oftentimes scared to guess wrong.

We all have different personalities and love languages—the way we prefer to give and receive love.[1] There are five main love languages, and every grieving mom's strongest language(s) will be different. For example, if *quality time* is your love language, your main desire may be for someone to sit and talk with you about your baby and grief journey. If *receiving gifts* is your love language, someone giving you a personalized present engraved with your baby's name would mean the world to you.

If *acts of service* is your love language, having someone pick up your groceries, cook you a meal, or clean your house may be what makes your day. For those who value *physical touch*, more hugs and arms around your shoulders might be needed to let you know someone cares. If *words of affirmation* is your love language, like it is mine, receiving a card in the mail or an encouraging text message from a friend may be what your heart needs.

Sharing your needs requires immense courage and vulnerability, so you should choose the right people to open up to. You don't need to bare your soul with every coworker or acquaintance (unless you want to). If you feel someone may not be receptive to your feedback or isn't a safe person to confide in, it's okay to refrain from doing so.

Also, some people may not follow through with what you ask of them—offering you yet another opportunity to practice using your Grace Cup. If this relationship is important to you, it's worth communicating and lovingly correcting them when needed.

The problem with assuming people know what we need, or being too passive in our communication with them, is that it leads to missed opportunities for support, which can lead to disappointment, resentment, and relational tension.

It's best to communicate clearly from the beginning to prevent this from happening. Instead of dropping hints, it's better to be specific and direct (in a kind and loving way, of course). Here are some examples of what you could say.

I've been struggling recently. (Share specifics here.) It would mean a lot to me if you would . . .

- Ask me how I'm doing.
- Talk about my baby.
- Spend time with me.
- Help me with . . . (picking up groceries, cleaning the house, doing laundry, watching my kids, bringing a meal over, etc.).

My baby's due date (or Heaven Day) is coming up on (date). I miss them so much, and it's been hard for me to imagine facing that day. It would be so helpful if you would . . .

- Remember and send me a text or card on that day to let me know you're thinking of me and my baby.
- Spend part of the day with me (go to lunch, meet at their grave, etc.).
- Do something special in memory of my baby (maybe you plan for friends and family to do random of acts of kindness, wear a certain color, or give a donation in their memory).
- Come to an event with me (perhaps you plan a memorial service, balloon release, Heavenly birthday party, or other gathering).

The holidays are approaching, and it makes me sad to think of spending Christmas (Thanksgiving, Easter, Mother's Day, etc.) without my baby. I would really appreciate if you would . . .

- Support and encourage me on that day.
- Remember my baby and include them in our family traditions.
  - Maybe you ask them to light a candle on the Thanksgiving table in memory of your baby, hang a stocking for them at Christmas, or find some other special way for your baby to be included in the holiday.
- Give me grace if I'm not myself or don't feel like participating like I normally do.
  - Maybe you choose to arrive late, leave early, or not attend at all; or maybe you don't partake in certain activities.

I'd also like to share some potential ways to gracefully respond to common remarks people make about pregnancy loss. You may not feel comfortable correcting others, but I want you to know that it's okay to lovingly educate people when they say something that isn't helpful or true (especially if it's someone close to you with whom you will have an ongoing relationship).

Using the Grace Cup may mean that you remain silent and say nothing at all, or it might involve using one of the responses below. I trust that the Holy Spirit will guide you in responding to each situation and person with truth, love, and grace.

Remark	Response
"At least you're young and can get pregnant again."	"I'm not sure if or when we are going to try again, but right now, I am grieving my baby who died (use your baby's name here if you named your baby). Whether we have more children or not, I will always love and miss this baby/ (baby's name). No future child will ever be able to replace him or her."
"You should be grateful you have living children." Or, "At least you have other children."	"I am grateful for all the children God gave me, but having children on earth doesn't ease the pain of losing this baby. I am grieving the hopes and dreams I had for this specific child. I am also sad that my other children will not get to know their sibling here on earth."
"God needed another angel." Or, "Your baby was too beautiful for earth."	"I don't believe God took my baby because He needed him/her or that my baby was too good for earth. Sadly, my baby died because of the brokenness of this world, but thankfully, I will see him/her again in Heaven. I don't believe my baby will be an angel in Heaven because he/she is a human. But that's a good thing because my baby will take part in the Resurrection and will receive a glorified body one day."
"Everything happens for a reason."	"I don't believe my baby's death was part of God's good plan because He hates death. But I do trust that God will bring purpose from my pain as I lean into Him for strength."

These are merely starting points. Of course, modify them to fit your needs, personal communication style, and specific relationships. If possible, it's best to communicate in person or over the phone rather than text or email, where tone and emotion can be misinterpreted.

• • • FRIENDSHIPS AND COMMUNITY • • •

Losing a baby can strain friendships. After Bridget went to Heaven, some of my friends didn't acknowledge my pain or her existence, and I found it hard to be close to them. Some expected me to move on and return to normal, which I could not do. As a result, I lost some friendships.

But I've lived long enough to know that friendships come and go. Some friends are for a lifetime, while others are for a season. Over time, all friendships change to some degree because life changes, and people do too. Losing a baby is a profound, life-altering event. It thrusts you into a new normal—one you never asked for but now must live with.

If you reflect on other significant life events, such as leaving home after high school, starting college, landing your first job, or getting married, you probably noticed that your friendships changed during those transitions. The same holds true when you've lost a baby. You're not the same person you were before. Your loss has significantly changed you, so it's likely that some of your friendships will also change.

It will sift your stronger friendships from the weaker ones. Though losing a baby shouldn't be treated as a friendship test, it will naturally reveal which friends are there for you and which ones aren't. Your stack of sympathy cards will hold the signatures of those who took the time to write you a note (and you will notice the lack of those who didn't).

Likewise, your Meal Train link will show you the names of those who took action (and those who didn't). You'll always remember those who sent a text, ran an errand, gave a gift card, or sent flowers. And likewise, you'll never forget those who didn't show up—either at all, or to the level you expected them to.

You will be tempted to focus on the people who let you down. You will ruminate over how little they did and how much they disappointed you. But my advice is to instead pay attention to the people who showed up. Take notice of the ones who went above and beyond, and also to the ones who pleasantly surprised you.

Losing Bridget caused me to grow closer to my true friends while drifting apart from those who weren't there for me. Though this process was painful, the outcome was ultimately for the best. The people in my life now are the ones who will stand by me through thick and thin, through the deepest valleys, not just the mountaintops. Isn't that what we truly desire in friendship?

An unexpected gift of grief was the rich and fulfilling friendships God formed as a result of my loss. Many of my closest friends now are fellow grieving mothers, whom I wouldn't have met if it weren't for Bridget. These friendships—born from shared vulnerability and heartache—are deeper and more satisfying than having surface-level acquaintances.

I met my first grieving mom friend through the cemetery. At Bridget's burial, we noticed a fresh grave to the left of hers and assumed that another family had recently lost a baby as well. A few weeks later, a temporary marker with the name Jack Monroe was placed on the grave, along with his parents' names.

I found his mom, Casey, on Facebook, and we talked for hours on the phone, connecting over our grief in a way that none of my other friends understood. She and I walked through all our first milestones together, from our babies' due dates and Heaven Days to the first Thanksgiving and Christmas and all the hard days in between.

We often visited Jack and Bridget's graves to replace their flowers, clean their headstones, and even have picnics together. During Christmas, we began a tradition of decorating small trees with solar-powered lights and ornaments and then staking them in the ground behind their headstones.

Casey and her family have been with me since the beginning of Bridget's Cradles and have faithfully supported the organization throughout the years. Serving with Casey and many other grieving mom friends is one of my favorite parts of ministry. There is nothing better than serving Jesus alongside your best friends!

Momma, I know people have hurt you, but the Lord will use people to heal you too. In your disappointment, don't be tempted to push people away. Isolating yourself in grief is exactly what the enemy wants you to do, making it easier for him to lead you astray. You *need* people now more than ever.

Community is the antidote for the loneliness you feel. You *can't* and *shouldn't* do this alone. Grieving with others is better than grieving alone. Let the Body of Christ weep with you and spur you on in your journey (Romans 12:15; Hebrews 10:24).

It's important to have sisters in Christ to remind you of the truth of His Word and offer you hope and encouragement on your darkest days. If you don't already have a community of believers and bereaved moms, here are some ideas on how to find them:

- Be engaged in your local church. Sign up for a women's event, Bible study, or grief support group (if your church offers one).

- Ask your pastor to connect you with other grieving moms in your congregation.

- Attend a Christ-centered pregnancy and infant loss support group in person or online. Bridget's Cradles offers a free support group, Hope Online, which I lead monthly. I would love to meet you there. You can sign up to attend our next one at BridgetsCradles.com/HopeOnline.

- Join a Christian pregnancy and infant loss Facebook group. Share your story, connect with other grieving moms, and find other hope-filled resources. We would love to welcome you to our *Cradled in Hope Facebook group* at Facebook.com/Groups/CradledInHope.

- Post your story on social media and ask grieving moms to contact you. You could also search for others' stories online. We share many stories on our blog.
- Contact the hospital where you delivered or the cemetery where your baby is buried. They may hold special events for grieving families or be able to connect you with local organizations.
- Attend a pregnancy and infant loss remembrance event in your community or state.
- Bridget's Cradles hosts *Wave of Light* in Wichita, Kansas, annually on October 15, Pregnancy and Infant Loss Remembrance Day. Families from other states attend. Although traveling to the event might not be possible for everyone, please know you are invited to join us.

• • • MY CUP RUNNETH OVER • • •

I want to close with one final cup analogy—this time from King David in Psalm 23. In the most famous psalm of the Bible, David portrays God as his Shepherd who takes care of all his needs. Even in the darkest valleys, David declares he will fear no evil because he knows God is with him.

He proclaims, "You prepare a table before me in the presence of my enemies. You anoint my head with oil; my cup overflows" (v. 5). The King James Version reads, "My cup runneth over." What cup is he referring to? Bible scholars surmise David used the cup as a metaphor to convey that God not only supplies for his needs but blesses him with more than he could ever need.

David, a shepherd himself, had filled many buckets with water to quench the thirst of his sheep. Perhaps one day, as the water from the buckets overflowed onto the pasture, he reflected on his life and the abundance God had given him.

Friend, I know your life cup is full right now, and you don't know if you can handle one more drop. Grief and all its heavy emotions have weighed you down. My prayer for you is that the Lord would empty your cup and refill it, overflowing, with the kind of water only He can provide.

Jesus told us the water He gives us will become in us "a spring of water welling up to eternal life" and "whoever drinks the water I give them will never thirst" (John 4:14). I pray the Lord will richly bless you with friendships, community, and His healing touch. May your cup run over, and you never thirst again.

Prayers to Heaven

Jesus, we come to You wounded by others' words. You have shown us extravagant grace by dying on the cross for us. Let us follow Your example and forgive those who have hurt us. Help us see the best in others and clearly communicate our hearts and needs to them. Strengthen our relationships and forge new friendships along the way. Surround us with a community of believers and fellow grieving moms who will carry our burden and point us toward You. Fill our cups to overflowing with Your water. Amen.

Truth to Cling To

Proverbs 17:17; Matthew 18:21–22; Mark 11:25; Luke 6:37; 1 Corinthians 13:4–5; Galatians 6:2; James 5:16

TIME WITH JESUS

1. Did you relate to the Tale of Two Cups? Are your emotions at the brim? How would adopting the Grace Cup mentality change that? Ask the Lord to give you a heart posture of grace and prepare you to pour it when hurtful words arise.
2. Have you been hurt by someone during this season of grief? Are you withholding forgiveness from them? Write a prayer to grant them forgiveness and thank Jesus for the forgiveness He has given you.
3. Have your friendships changed after losing a baby? Reflect on each friendship: What happened or changed? How does it make you feel? How will you respond, based on what you learned in this chapter?

HEALING STEPS

1. Reflect on your love languages and contemplate what you need from others right now. Reach out to someone who comes to mind and express your needs to them. Use my examples on pages 143–144 as a starting point if you want.
2. Meet with a close, trusted friend and share your heart. Practice vulnerability, and don't hold back your tears. Share the deepest, hardest parts of what you're feeling.
3. Choose one idea from the list on pages 148–149 to connect with a support community and form friendships with other grieving moms. Have lunch or coffee with someone, sign up for Hope Online, or join our Facebook group.

9

The Good Fight

WHEN YOU ENCOUNTER
THE ENEMY'S ATTACKS

Fight the good fight of the faith. Take hold of the eternal life to
which you were called when you made your good confession in
the presence of many witnesses.

1 Timothy 6:12

Trigger Warning: medical trauma

Five weeks before Bridget's birth // "Nothing good will ever come
from this," I uttered under my breath while sitting on the edge of
my bed. I needed to tell God, out loud, just how dire my situation
had become and how little I thought He would do to redeem it.

My feeble vocal cords broke the silence in the darkness of my
bedroom, which had been my prison for the last six weeks. Closed
blinds dampened the daylight and shut me into the shadows of
my hopeless thoughts.

I slowly stood up and made my way to the toilet, which had become an unwelcome friend in what was supposed to be a happy and healthy first pregnancy. I changed my pad and watched blood drip into the toilet, pooling crimson at the bottom.

How could I be losing this much blood and still be alive? How can my baby still be alive? Why is my body doing this to my baby? I snapped a picture on my phone of the blood-filled toilet bowl to show my OB. Maybe if I documented it as evidence, she would understand just how severe and scary it was for me to be bleeding this much every day.

Does she care? Does anyone understand how hopeless this situation feels? I felt utterly alone in my misery, as if I was going to become just another statistic of a patient with a subchorionic hemorrhage who would end up miscarrying her baby. After all, it's common: One in four pregnancies ends in loss. But this was anything but commonplace to me. My whole world was crashing down as every hope and dream for my daughter's life was being shattered right in front of me.

I carefully walked over to my bathroom sink to wash my hands, and I caught my reflection in the mirror. Weeks of bed rest had lent itself to showerless days of no makeup and messy ponytails. This wasn't how I pictured carrying my first child—being holed up in my house for endless days of wearing sweatpants and T-shirts.

I only left my home for doctor's appointments and one trip to a store as my mom pushed me around in a wheelchair. My depressing reality was far from the pregnancy glow I had dreamed of experiencing all my life. I locked eyes with my own in the mirror and watched as tears welled up and fell down my cheeks.

Built-up emotional pain escaped, demanding I feel the weight of everything I had been carrying. I couldn't bottle up or push down my emotions any longer. All at once, all my fears and insecurities came rushing to the surface when I heard a voice say: "You're not good enough to be a mom. God's not going to save your baby."

There it was. The unthinkable worst-case scenario planted in my mind by the great deceiver, Satan. Though the voice sounded like mine, I knew the message was coming from him. Who else would want to make me feel unworthy to be a mother? Who else would desire to lead me away from my Savior and make me question God's intentions for me?

And his tactics worked—at least temporarily. During my days on bed rest, I felt as though God had abandoned me. I wondered, *What have I done to deserve this? Am I being punished? Why can other women, ones who don't even want their babies, have healthy pregnancies? Why is God allowing my body to be an unsafe place for my daughter to live and grow?*

I lay back down and cried out to God, "Why me? Where are You?" Overwhelmed by my grief and the unfairness of it all, the enemy used my pain to tempt me to mistrust God. He whispered his lies: *If God is good, why isn't He good to you? Surely God wouldn't let you suffer like this if He really loved you. See, God's not answering your prayers! He left you when you needed Him the most.*

These seeds of doubt eventually grew, making me feel abandoned and unloved by God. What if the enemy was right? Can God *really* love me and let me lose my daughter? If He knew what was best for me, He surely wouldn't let *this* be a part of my life story. What about you, my friend? Has the enemy planted similar lies and made you feel forsaken by God?

• • • WHO SHOULD I BLAME? • • •

During a support group meeting, I posed some thought-provoking questions to the grieving moms surrounding me: "We are quick to blame God for the loss of our babies. But why don't we blame Satan instead—isn't he the reason death exists? Shouldn't we direct our anger toward him instead of God?"

The questions stimulated an insightful discussion and led to an interesting theory: We don't blame Satan because we don't have a relationship with him. Since we have a relationship with God, we tend to hold Him responsible. Because God is all-powerful, we believe He could have, and should have, saved our babies. Since He didn't, we point the finger at Him.

In our opinion, He sat back and let this happen. He didn't intervene. We trusted Him to answer our prayers and protect our babies, but He didn't. Why didn't He heal my subchorionic hemorrhage or breathe life back into Bridget's lungs? Or better yet, why did He allow me to have pregnancy complications to begin with?

Have you ever struggled with this endless blame game? In this chapter, we will settle the debate and look at who is actually responsible for pregnancy and infant loss: the enemy. We will learn about who he is, how he works, and how to fight against his evil schemes.

So let's start with these two crucial questions: Who is he, and where did he come from? Most people think the first sin happened in the Garden of Eden when Eve took a bite of the forbidden fruit after being tempted by Satan (Genesis 3:1–14). However, the first sin actually occurred before that.

Lucifer (Satan's name before his fall) was God's "anointed guardian cherub," whom God called the "signet of perfection" (Ezekiel 28:12–19 ESV). Being a beautiful angel adorned in precious stones, Lucifer became prideful and desired to be more powerful than God. He was filled with sin and violence, and God cast him out of the "mountain of God" (Ezekiel 28:16 ESV; Isaiah 14:12–14). Jesus, who has always existed, witnessed Lucifer "fall like lightning" from Heaven (Luke 10:18 ESV).

In addition, a third of the angels joined Lucifer in his disobedience to God and fell with him (Revelation 12:4). These fallen angels are now known as demons or unclean spirits. Satan leads these spiritual forces of darkness. He is known as the "ruler of this world" and the "prince of the power of the air" (John 14:30; Ephesians 2:2 ESV).

Satan is the "god of this world [who] has blinded the minds of the unbelievers, to keep them from seeing the light of the gospel of the glory of Christ" (2 Corinthians 4:4 ESV). Though he is powerful and can wreak devastation, he is no match for Jesus, who died on the cross so that "through death, he might destroy the one who has the power of death, that is, the devil" (Hebrews 2:14 ESV).

God will one day throw Satan into the Lake of Fire forever (Revelation 20:10). Victory is coming! However, knowing Satan currently rules this earth gives us a heightened perspective on the current state of affairs in the world and the personal battles we face.

Paul declared, "Our struggle is not against flesh and blood, but against the rulers, against the authorities, against the powers of this dark world and against the spiritual forces of evil in the heavenly realms" (Ephesians 6:12).

• • • STEAL, KILL, AND DESTROY • • •

I hesitated to devote an entire chapter to discussing Satan. But it's essential to address the spiritual battles we encounter as grieving mothers. When we lose a baby, our hearts are broken, and our walls are down. Grief can weaken even the strongest faith, and the enemy rejoices to see us in this frail, vulnerable state.

Peter warned us that our adversary, the devil, is like a roaring lion always "seeking whom he may devour" (1 Peter 5:8 KJV). Just as lions prey on weak and wounded animals, the enemy perceives a grieving mother as an easy victim to attack, especially if she is alone and isolated.

Think of it from his sick and twisted perspective. The loss of your baby is an ideal scenario in which he can wreak havoc on your faith. The stage is set for you to doubt God. You are wallowing in sorrow and questioning why God would allow this to happen to you. Your faith may be hanging on by a thread—perfect timing for the enemy to cut the final string.

Satan desires to snatch away what is sown in your heart (Matthew 13:19) and use your grief against you. Even worse than that, He wants to use your grief to pit you *against God*! The enemy will do anything in his power to turn your heart away from your Creator.

While grief is a sensitive time to listen to God's voice, it's also a time when we are susceptible to believing the lies whispered by the enemy. Jesus told us, "The thief comes only to steal and kill and destroy" (John 10:10). Satan's mission for the grieving mother is to:

- *steal* her joy
- *kill* her relationships with God and others
- *destroy* her life and hope for the future

Though death has temporarily separated you from your baby, Satan's ultimate goal is to separate you permanently from your baby and God. He wants you to miss out on the glorious hope of Heaven. As God's enemy, he wants to lead as many souls as he can to Hell in utter defiance of God. But how does he persuade people to choose eternal damnation?

It's not by convincing them that what he offers is better than what God offers. No logical or emotional argument could entice someone to trade eternal glory for eternal torment. Very few people, if any, would willingly choose to live forever in a fiery place with Satan over a beautiful Paradise with God Himself. Instead, the enemy uses deception to trick people into forsaking God's gift of salvation.

Satan is the father of lies, and there is no truth in him (John 8:44). He is cunning, conniving, and manipulative. Even if he fails to persuade you to renounce your faith or reject Jesus, he will still try to ruin your life and create chaos in your mind. Some of the tactics Satan uses to achieve his goals are to:

- Convince you that he is not real and that Hell is not a real place
- Persuade you that there is no God or make you indifferent toward Him
- Manipulate you into believing Jesus is not who He claimed to be
- Make you believe God is not good and that He has abandoned you
- Confuse you about God's character and cause you to doubt Him
- Twist God's Word to lead you astray
- Tempt you to turn to sin and worldly coping mechanisms to heal your heart
- Isolate you and disconnect you from the Body of Christ
- Cause tension in your marriage and relationships
- Lead you to ruminate on your past and become fearful of your future
- Provoke you to become obsessive and controlling

It can be difficult to recognize the enemy's tactics because he often disguises them in crafty ways. Satan is a master of deception and "masquerades as an angel of light" (2 Corinthians 11:14). The devil doesn't show up wearing horns and holding a pitchfork; he is far smarter than that.

Satan knows Scripture and mixes his lies with the truth. In my despair after losing Bridget, he made me question whether I had somehow fallen out of favor with God and was now living outside of His will. I wondered if I had done something wrong to deserve to lose my baby.

Anxiety plagued me as I searched for the answer to the most significant question every bereaved mom wants to know: *Why did this happen to me?* There's a biblical explanation to that question, which we've discussed throughout this book, but Satan has his own counterfeit answers: *You did this to your baby*, or, *God did this to you.*

The enemy exploits this *why* question with all his might. He wants to use your loss to make you feel unloved, unworthy, and abandoned by God. Satan tries to reshape your core beliefs about God by planting rotten seeds in your heart, knowing they will turn into spoiled fruit.

Rotten Seeds (from the enemy)	Spoiled Fruit
confusion, doubt, condemnation, fear, temptation	guilt, regret, resentment, shame, bitterness, anger, anxiety, depression, negative attitude, victim mentality, controlling personality, sin, addiction

We need to recognize these unwelcome emotions as the side effects of believing the enemy's lies. They are not from God! Our Heavenly Father always speaks love, grace, and hope over us. He sows good seeds in our hearts, and as a result, we bear the fruit of the Spirit: "love, joy, peace, forbearance, kindness, goodness, faithfulness, gentleness and self-control" (Galatians 5:22–23). We can determine the source of the seeds by the fruit they produce.

• • • WE ARE AT WAR • • •

When I was young, I used to think God and Satan symbolically perched on my shoulders as if the devil were always present, tempting me at every opportunity. However, Satan is not omnipresent like God, which means he cannot be everywhere at once.

This is a comforting thought because it is unlikely Satan himself is personally bothering me or you. I imagine he spends most of his time stirring up world leaders to fuel hatred, corruption, deception, and wars. Though I won't claim to know his personal schedule or current location, I do know he roams the earth (Job 1:7), and his demons are the ones who help him carry out his evil schemes.

Although it may seem intimidating to study Satan and his demons, it is crucial to understand how they fight so we can resist them. When nations are at war, militaries gather intelligence on their enemies to gain an advantage. Basic information, such as enemy army size, weapons, and tactics, is crucial for military leaders before sending troops into battle.

Friend, we are at war. Earth is a spiritual battleground for the eternal state of our souls. We need to know how to combat the spiritual forces of darkness that wage war against us. The Bible contains frequent war language, particularly in the New Testament and Paul's letters to the Church.

For instance, Paul encouraged us to join him in suffering to become good *soldiers* of Jesus Christ (2 Timothy 2:3). He told us to be "strong in the Lord and in his mighty power" and to "put on the full armor of God, so that you can take your stand against the devil's schemes" (Ephesians 6:10–11). Armor is meant to protect and defend.

• • • THE ARMOR OF GOD • • •

- Belt of truth
- Breastplate of righteousness
- Feet fitted with the Gospel of peace
- Shield of faith
- Helmet of salvation
- Sword of the Spirit

Notice how each piece intentionally guards our hearts, minds, and bodies; for example, the shield of faith is meant to "extinguish all the flaming arrows of the evil one" (Ephesians 6:16–17). However, there is one piece that is *both* a defensive and offensive weapon: the sword of the Spirit, which is the Word of God (v. 17).

If we submit to God and resist the devil, he will flee from us (James 4:7). So, if you sense you are under spiritual attack, call on the name of Jesus. Unlike God, Satan and his demons cannot read our thoughts. They study our outward behavior and habits to predict our thought patterns and predilections. Thankfully, they do not have access to the sacred space of our minds. So, if you want to tell the demons to flee, you need to say Jesus' powerful name *out loud*!

• • • THE SHEPHERD'S VOICE • • •

Discerning between God's voice and the enemy's voice necessitates more than mere knowledge about God. It calls for a deep, personal relationship with Him. Even demons believe in the one true God (James 2:19). In John 10, the same chapter in which Jesus warned us about the enemy coming as a thief, Jesus described Himself as the Good Shepherd, who lays down His life for His sheep.

He said, "My sheep listen to my voice; I know them, and they follow me" (v. 27). To better appreciate Jesus' metaphor, let's imagine the life of a shepherd in biblical Israel. Shepherds usually lived nomadically and spent their days under the scorching sun, leading their flock to water sources and to green pastures where the animals could graze on fresh grass.

Shepherds took short naps during the day to remain alert at night and protect their flock from predators. In the winter months, they endured cold temperatures. David, one of the most prominent figures and shepherds in the Bible, killed both a lion and a bear with his own hands to rescue sheep from their mouths (1 Samuel 17:34–36).

You can see why sheep would follow the voice of their shepherd. From their point of view, they have formed a deep trust and familiarity with him. He feeds and takes care of them. They have seen him fend off predators to keep them safe. Therefore, when he speaks to them, they follow his commands, knowing he has their protection and best interest at heart.

The same is true for us as we follow our Good Shepherd. The more we see how He tends and cares for us, the more we trust Him. The longer we walk with Him, the more familiar we are with His voice. Over the years, I've seen various charts online similar to the one below. I created this one for you because I have found the side-by-side comparison a valuable tool in my faith journey.[1]

God's Voice	The Enemy's Voice
Calms	Worries
Comforts	Controls
Convicts	Condemns, Shames
Encourages	Discourages
Enlightens/Educates	Confuses
Heals	Hurts
Leads	Pushes
Reassures	Frightens, Threatens
Soothes	Obsesses
Stills	Rushes
Strengthens	Weakens

"God is not a God of confusion" (1 Corinthians 14:33 ESV). He is not deceptive, sneaky, or manipulative. He never tempts us to sin, unlike Satan, who tailors our temptations to our tendencies. God will not speak defeating words over your identity. He will not condemn or shame you. Most importantly, God's voice never—ever—contradicts His character or His Word.

Therefore, if you have a thought (or someone tells you something) that contradicts who God is in Scripture, you can be sure the message is not from Him! Here are some questions to help you determine if a message is from God or the enemy:

- Does it align with Scripture?
- Is it characteristic of God's nature?
- What is the general purpose behind it?
- What does it make me want to do?
- Will this lead me to sin?
- Is it bringing me closer to God or pulling me further from Him?
- Is this conviction or condemnation?

Taking time to pray and reflect can help you discern the enemy's lies. Messages from God will always pass the Philippians 4:8 test, where Paul instructed us to think about things that are true, noble, right, pure, lovely, admirable, excellent, and praiseworthy.

If it doesn't pass the test, we reject the lie in Jesus' name and combat it with Truth! This simple practice can be life-changing if we let it impact our thinking. Instead of dwelling on the enemy's disparaging deception, we focus on the never-failing, hope-filled promises of God's Word.

Thoughts/Lies	Truth	Scripture Support
I am not a good mom. I should have saved my baby.	I am a good mom. I would have saved my baby if I could have.	"Therefore, there is now no condemnation for those who are in Christ Jesus." Romans 8:1
God must be punishing me. He abandoned me. God doesn't love me.	God is with me. He hasn't left me. God loves me.	"See what great love the Father has lavished on us, that we should be called children of God!" 1 John 3:1 "God has said, 'Never will I leave you; never will I forsake you.'" Hebrews 13:5

I want to close this chapter with some comforting words from Isaiah 40:11, a prophecy about the coming Messiah's tender heart for the vulnerable, specifically for mothers and babies:

> He tends his flock like a shepherd:
>> He gathers the lambs in his arms
> and carries them close to his heart;
>> he gently leads those that have young.

While this verse does not mention the loss of a child, I can feel Jesus' compassion for moms and their children as He carries them close to His heart. Can you imagine the depth of His love for a grieving mother like yourself? He is your Good Shepherd, cradling your baby and you like the lamb and ewe. Oh, I pray you will know and follow His voice all the days of your life.

PRAYERS TO HEAVEN

Jesus, thank You for dying on the cross to defeat the enemy! We rejoice that You have the ultimate victory over sin and death. But right now, we are weak and wounded. We need You to defend us from the enemy's attacks. In our season of grief, we can sense him trying to "steal, kill, and destroy." Help us put on the armor of God and fight back. Teach us to discern Your voice from the lies of the enemy. Thank You for being our Good Shepherd. We will follow You where You lead us. Amen.

TRUTH TO CLING TO

Isaiah 35:4; Luke 10:19; Romans 16:20; 1 Corinthians 15:55–57; Colossians 2:15; 1 John 3:8; Revelation 12:9

TIME WITH JESUS

1. Which tactics on page 159 is the enemy using on you? How will you combat these spiritual attacks in the future?
2. Are there signs of spoiled fruit in your life? Trace the spoiled fruit back to the rotten seeds Satan may have planted in your heart.
3. Identify a lie of the enemy you've been believing and reject it in Jesus' name. Fill out the chart in your *CIH Guided Journal* to claim God's Truth over the lie.

HEALING STEPS

1. Print our Fruits of the Spirit page from your *CIH Guided Journal*. Frame it and place it somewhere to remind you that Jesus will sow good seeds in the soil of your heart.
2. Fill out the Armor of God chart in your *CIH Guided Journal*. Write down each piece of armor, and imagine yourself being covered in it, protected from the enemy.
3. The next time you are confronted with a spiritual attack, say this out loud: "In the name of Jesus, I command Satan and his demons to flee!" Remember, Satan doesn't have access to your thoughts.

10

A Renewed Mind

WHEN YOU ARE ANXIOUS OR TRIGGERED

When my anxieties multiply,
Your comforting calms me down.

Psalm 94:19 CEB

You're in the checkout lane at a store when you notice a pregnant woman in front of you. You look down at the conveyor belt and see baby items inching toward the clerk. With each beep of the scanner, your heart races faster. You feel hot as tears well up in the corners of your eyes.

You muster a smile, but on the inside, your deep grief rises to the surface. You think of your baby and the fact that you are no longer pregnant with them. As the clerk bags each item for the expectant mother, you think: *I won't ever get to zip up my baby's footed pajamas or pick out a cute onesie for them to wear. They'll never play with toys or drink from a bottle.*

You want to cry but hold the tears back until you get to your car. You drive home with tears streaming down your face. You miss your baby so much. This unexpected encounter at the store has derailed your whole day and caused sadness to linger in your heart.

• • • TRIGGER WARNING • • •

As much as I wish you hadn't experienced a situation like this, I assume you probably have. Maybe you sat next to a baby at church. Or saw a pregnancy announcement on social media. Or a message popped up from your pregnancy app telling you that your baby is now the size of a mango. Except you're not pregnant anymore, and this untimely notification feels like a dagger straight to your heart.

These stressful situations can plunge your heart into an emotional tailspin. Whether you are in the first months of fresh grief or years into your healing journey, these unexpected triggers lurk in everyday situations and can wreak havoc on your emotions.

If you've been in a pregnancy loss group online, you've probably seen a post shared with the phrase **TW** (which stands for Trigger Warning). This label announces to potential readers that it references something that could upset them. For example: **TW: Living Children Mentioned** or **TW: Current Pregnancy Mentioned**. In groups of fellow grieving moms, the standard is to be extra sensitive in what is said and how it is shared. Unfortunately, the real world doesn't warn us of potential heartache looming ahead.

What are triggers? The definition of a trigger is "something that evokes the memory of a traumatic experience, setting off an intense negative emotional reaction."[1] This could cause feelings of anxiety, panic, and sadness. There are three types of triggers: *past*, *present*, and *future* (or *anticipatory*). Check the boxes next to the ones you have previously experienced or are currently facing. Are there other triggers I didn't list that are impacting you? Write them down in the blank spaces provided.

PAST TRIGGERS

- ☐ Reliving your baby's birth experience, death, funeral, or other traumatic event related to your loss (such as the moment you found out your baby no longer had a heartbeat at your doctor's office, handing your baby over to the nurse at the hospital for the last time, closing their casket, or burying them)
- ☐ Obsessively replaying the what-ifs and should-have-dones of your pregnancy (e.g., *What if I had noticed sooner that she stopped kicking? I shouldn't have eaten (this) or done (that). Maybe my baby would have lived if . . .*)
- ☐ _____

PRESENT TRIGGERS

- ☐ Seeing a pregnant woman or newborn baby
- ☐ Watching a close friend, family member, or coworker announce their pregnancy or have a due date around the time you were supposed to have your baby
- ☐ Seeing a child the same gender as the baby you lost at the age they would have been if they had lived
- ☐ Walking by baby aisles in stores or seeing advertisements for baby items
- ☐ Getting formula samples in the mail
- ☐ Receiving baby registry emails
- ☐ Being invited to a baby shower or gender reveal party
- ☐ Witnessing baby dedications or baptisms at church
- ☐ Having an appointment at your OB's office or the hospital where you gave birth (or even driving by it)
- ☐ Hearing people talk about their pregnancies or living children

☐ Talking with someone who doesn't acknowledge the loss of your baby or who says something insensitive

☐ Spending time in your baby's finished (or unfinished) nursery with all the clothes and items you had for them (or conversely, wishing the room wasn't so empty)

☐ Going to the bathroom and/or having your period again (bleeding can be incredibly triggering if you suffered a miscarriage or experienced pregnancy complications such as a subchorionic hemorrhage)

☐ Needing to wear maternity clothes because they still fit (or conversely, having to pack them away because you no longer need them)

☐ Being engorged from your milk coming in and then needing to choose whether you will dry up or pump and donate (both the presence and absence of breast milk are painful reminders that your baby is not here with you)

☐ _____

FUTURE / ANTICIPATORY TRIGGERS

☐ Assuming you will see pregnant women or babies if you go out in public (church, store, social events, work, etc.)

☐ Worrying about how someone will treat you in a particular situation or environment; for example, *If I go to (location/event), no one will talk to me about my baby or acknowledge my loss,* or *I don't think (person's name) will text me on my baby's due date.*

☐ Fretting over how you will handle a situation, e.g., *If I attend (event), I know I will be too sad and need to leave.*

☐ Dreading upcoming holidays or milestones such as your baby's due date or first birthday/Heaven Day and believing those days will be too hard for you to face

☐ _____

Which types of triggers are you struggling with the most? Let's now discuss how to cope with them.

• • • PROTECTING YOUR HEART • • •

When we suffer from a broken heart, we should treat it with the same care and attention we would give a physical injury. If you fractured a limb, you would use casts and crutches to protect it from further injury, giving it time to heal. In the same way, you should guard your heart against additional pain while the Lord heals you.

But bandages and gauze won't help with the emotional wound of losing a baby. We need a different set of protective measures. The psalmist David declared, "The Lord is my strength and my shield; my heart trusts in him, and he helps me" (Psalm 28:7). I love the visual of the Lord being our shield and surrounding us like a fortress.

Though Jesus safeguards our hearts, we can help Him by creating optimal conditions for His healing work. Here are some boundaries you may need to put in place *temporarily* to nurture your broken heart:

- Adjust your schedule to make time for grieving and being with Jesus.
- Avoid certain places, situations, or events that make you anxious.
- Reduce interactions with people who trigger you.
- Prepare for situations in advance.

After losing Bridget, I decided to leave a women's Bible study group I had been attending since before my pregnancy with her. Most of the women in the group were pregnant or nursing mothers. It was too hard for me to be the only mom in the group without a baby in her belly or arms during that fresh season of my grief.

I politely excused myself from the Bible study, and they were all gracious and understanding of my decision. It was nothing personal against them, and leaving the group didn't mean I would never be in another women's Bible study. It just meant that *right after my baby died* was not the right time for me.

Don't feel guilty for doing what you need to do to get through this season. With time and God's healing, you will once again be around pregnant women without feeling jealous or bitter. One day, a baby's laughter will bring you joy instead of reminding you of your sadness. You will be able to attend a friend's baby shower and rejoice for the precious new life God has given her instead of wanting to hide in a bathroom and cry.

As Christians who value the sanctity of human life, we *want* to celebrate the gift of new life for others, and we will. These triggers will not always bother you the way they do now. I promise it will get better! But in the meantime, don't let the enemy shame you into thinking it's wrong to shelter your heart while Jesus is healing you.

As women, we often feel guilty or selfish for saying no. But the word *no* can actually bring the freedom and healing we need in this season. What do you need to say no to? Do you need to unfollow or mute someone on social media? Get off social media altogether? A social media fast can be a very healthy discipline, especially while grieving. You may need to change doctor's offices, unsubscribe from certain email communications, and delete some apps.

Maybe you need to say no to attending specific social gatherings. Let's imagine a friend invites you to their baby shower. You're happy for them, but you know it's too soon for you to go. Instead of attending, tell your friend you want to support them, but you're hurting too much and don't think you can muster up the strength.

Have your husband or another friend purchase something from their registry for you. Send a card in advance and a text on the day of their shower. This way, you can let them know you're thinking of them without putting yourself in a situation that will cause you unnecessary grief.

Check in with your emotions daily. How do you feel today? Is it a good or bad day? As you know, grief has its ups and downs, and today can look very different than yesterday. You can evaluate your emotional state each day to determine what you feel up to doing.

For example, you could handle a baby shower invitation this way: Let your friend know you *might* attend, but it will depend on how you feel that day. You could send a gift and card ahead of time in case you end up not making it. This approach lets your feelings lead but also sets up boundaries that protect you and your friendship.

I promise you won't live like this forever. Even though it feels like your grief will never end, this season is temporary. Give yourself grace as you set these boundaries, and know it's impossible to avoid every person, place, or situation that causes you stress. Learning how to confront these triggers with new reactions is essential. With the Holy Spirit's guidance, you'll eventually react to triggers with peace rather than debilitating anxiety.

• • • AMYGDALA HIJACK • • •

There is a brain phenomenon behind our emotional responses to triggers. Buried deep in the middle of your brain are small almond-shaped collections of neurons called the amygdalae (plural here because you have two, one in each cerebral hemisphere).[2] Located inside the temporal lobe, the amygdala is "primarily involved in the processing of emotions and memories associated with fear."[3]

It is part of the limbic system and helps us process intense emotions.[4] The amygdala regulates the fight, flight, or freeze response[5] and immediately responds to perceived threats or triggers. Then, the prefrontal cortex in your frontal lobe is supposed to calm down the amygdala, allowing you to react rationally.

But an "amygdala hijack" happens when a strong emotion "impairs the prefrontal cortex" and overrides rational thought.[6] This results in an "intense emotional reaction that is out of proportion to the circumstance."[7] Has this happened to you before?

These reactions usually have physical side effects: a pit in your stomach, tight chest, shortness of breath, or difficulty falling or staying asleep. It could also manifest itself in other ways, like racing thoughts, a quick temper, irritability, uncontrollable anger, out-of-character words, paranoia, nightmares, irrational fear, or a general feeling of loss of control.

When people hear the term PTSD (post-traumatic stress disorder), they often associate it with combat veterans who have returned from war. However, this diagnosis can apply to anyone who has experienced a traumatic event and faces unwanted repercussions in their everyday life.

We should not downplay the trauma of suffering a miscarriage, delivering a stillborn baby, or losing an infant. The death of a child, no matter how many weeks or months old, is one of the most traumatic experiences a person can endure on this earth.

God did not create women to birth death. In God's original good design, babies were not supposed to die, and mothers' brains were not meant to process the trauma of losing them. This inherent PTSD provokes ramifications in the brain, including a hyperactive amygdala.[8]

This means that when a mother experiences the trauma of losing her baby, her amygdala is in a state of shock, which makes her even more susceptible to triggers. So, how do we break free from this vicious cycle? Let's focus now on how to calm our brains so God can heal our hearts.

• • • GROUNDED IN GOD • • •

Anxiety stems from fixating our thoughts on either the *past* or the *future*. Perseverating over the past or obsessively worrying about the future makes us feel a loss of control. To alleviate anxiety and calm the amygdala, we need to be grounded in the *present* moment.

The world defines *grounding* as a technique that keeps someone in the present and reorients them to the here-and-now of reality.[9] However, I believe we should be *grounded in God*, kept in God's presence, and reoriented to His now-and-forever Truth. Instead of being tossed to and fro by the *world*, we want to be anchored in His *Word*.

Before I continue, I want to issue a warning here. I have noticed some dangerous practices being introduced in the realm of pregnancy loss in recent years. The enemy has infiltrated the space and is luring grieving moms with promises of healing. Some of these practices are overtly occult, while others may seem harmless but are not.

Many of these healing practices do not have Christian origins and can lead you down a path of darkness. One of the most concerning trends I frequently see is people dabbling in New Age practices and worshiping created things in their pursuit of healing. Stay far away from crystals, tarot cards, palm readers, Ouija boards, psychics, mediums, astrology, and even yoga.

Steer clear even if people falsely advertise them as Christian, such as a "Christian medium" or "Christian yoga." I can assure you, there is no such thing. Engaging in these practices is like dancing with the devil. They are gateways to the demonic. Mediums promise you the opportunity to speak to your baby "on the other side." But God sternly warns us against using mediums and talking to the dead (Leviticus 19:31; 20:6); He refers to these practices as "detestable" (Deuteronomy 18:12).

While trying popular trends might be tempting, know that you will never find true healing apart from Jesus. He is the only One who can heal your heart (Psalm 147:3) and the only Mediator between us and God (1 Timothy 2:5). Our focus should be on Jesus in all aspects of healing. Simple exercises can help us remain grounded in Him.

One common technique is deep breathing. When you're in a state of amygdala hijack, your body's natural response is for your heart to beat faster and your breathing rate to quicken.[10] To combat this and to relax your body, take deep breaths from your diaphragm—in through your nose, out through your mouth. As you do so, pray to Jesus and repeat hope-filled Bible verses, such as:

- "Even though I walk through the valley of the shadow of death, I will fear no evil, for you are with me" (Psalm 23:4 ESV).
- "Truly he is my rock and my salvation; he is my fortress, I will never be shaken" (Psalm 62:2).
- "Weeping may stay for the night, but rejoicing comes in the morning" (Psalm 30:5).

Here are some additional ways to ground yourself in God:

WORSHIP

Turn on worship music with biblically sound lyrics. Listen to old hymns. Lift your hands or place them in front of you, palms up, in a posture of surrender. Release your burdens to Jesus. If you can't muster the strength to sing out loud, let the words wash over you. There is power in praising Jesus in the middle of your pain.

SCRIPTURE MEMORY

Print out Bible verses on cards (or buy Scripture memory cards). Keep them in your purse, nightstand drawer, or car console and pull them out when anxious thoughts flood in.

Moses told the Israelites to tie God's commandments to their hands and write them on the doorframes of their houses (Deuteronomy 6:8–9). We should do the same! You can display Bible verses on your bathroom mirror, computer desk, or other places you will see them frequently.

Commit verses to memory. There are many ways to do this, including using Bible memory apps, writing them on note cards, saying them out loud, writing out the first letter of each word, or putting them to songs. Change the lock screen on your phone to be your memory verse for the week. Hiding God's Word in your heart will keep you grounded in His Truth.

· · · REPEATING SCRIPTURE AFFIRMATIONS · · · AND BIBLICAL SELF-TALK

Repeat these truth-filled declarations (or make your own) when the enemy's lies creep in and cause anxiety:

- God loves me. He is with me. God will not abandon me. He will get me through this.
- My baby is in Heaven. We will not be separated forever. I will spend eternity with them.
- If I could have saved my baby, I would have. Their death is not my fault. I love my baby. I am a good mom.
- *If you find yourself comparing your life to someone else's*: That's their season, not mine. God is writing a different story for me. He promises a hope-filled future for me.

• • • VISUAL BIBLICAL IMAGERY • • •

In times of panic, I find it helpful to visualize being in Jesus' physical presence, even though His Holy Spirit is already inside me. It gives me peace to think of Bridget being safe in Jesus' presence too.

- Imagine Jesus holding your hand or standing next to you with His arm around your shoulder.
- Envision angels surrounding you, both ahead and behind you. If you're anxious at night, imagine angels at your bedposts watching over you.
- Visualize a beautiful place where you can meet with Jesus, perhaps a favorite place you've visited or what you imagine Heaven to be like.
- Picture Jesus holding your baby in His arms in Heaven. Or envision your child at another age sitting on Jesus' lap or exploring the wonders of Heaven (e.g., your daughter running through a field of flowers or your son climbing a tree).
- Imagine your reunion with your baby in Heaven. Think of the moment you are finally reunited in glorified bodies and will never be separated again. Envision a big, beautiful hug and play that wonderful scene over and over again in your mind!

• • • A RENEWED MIND • • •

Jesus desires to replace our panic with His peace. As Paul told the Romans, "Do not conform to the pattern of this world, but be transformed by the *renewing of your mind*" (Romans 12:2, emphasis added). A transformation is needed to retrain our brains to override their instinctive patterns.

Anxiety and depression are patterns of this fallen world. However, as believers, we have the power to overcome them! Before His arrest, Jesus washed His disciples' feet and assured them His Spirit would always be with them. He said, "Peace I leave with you; my peace I give you. I do not give to you as the world gives. Do not let your hearts be troubled and do not be afraid" (John 14:27).

Jesus revealed a hidden gift in verse 27—His peace—imparted through the Holy Spirit to comfort and strengthen His followers in times of hardship. Read Philippians 4:6–7. Paul said by "prayer and petition," we receive God's peace that guards our hearts and minds. Prayer is the master key to unlocking His peace.

In times of anxiety, are you scrolling on your phone instead of praying? Are you reaching for food instead of your Bible? I must admit, I have done both. But seeking comfort in worldly solutions will always leave you empty and unsatisfied. Instead, your first response should be to turn to God in prayer. Maintain a conversation with Him throughout your day.

Talk to Him more than you would your best friend! Though we don't have God's personal phone number to text or call Him (don't you wish He had one?), we do have a direct line of communication through prayer. And the best part is that He is available 24/7 to listen and talk with us. He wants to hear our hearts and comfort us in our chaos.

So, as triggers arise, let's first go to Him. Better yet, let's go to Him *before* they present themselves. Remember the anticipatory triggers we discussed earlier in this chapter and how we expect negative emotional responses before we even experience them?

My hope is that you'll learn to *anticipate* God's peace before a trigger even arises! I'll be honest: There were many moments I once dreaded and feared would be too difficult to face, such as Bridget's due date, her first Heaven Day, and the first Christmas without her. But they all eventually came to pass, and I found that the anticipation of the hard day was worse than the day itself.

Jesus was with me, and His peace sustained me. I know He will help me through future trials because I have learned to trust in His faithfulness. He carried me through before; I know He'll do it again. Exercising faith in Jesus is like strengthening a spiritual muscle. Turning to Him during distressing moments becomes more natural with practice.

However, if you are feeling hopeless and having suicidal thoughts, please seek help immediately. Tell someone how you're feeling and make an appointment with a licensed counselor or psychiatrist. I highly recommend seeing a Christian counselor trained in EMDR (*Eye Movement Desensitization and Reprocessing*) therapy—which research has shown to be very successful in treating PTSD.

Do you feel uneasy or embarrassed about going to counseling? Let me assure you that receiving therapy is a sign of strength, not weakness. I have seen a counselor throughout many seasons of my life and currently see mine weekly. Having a safe place to process my emotions helps me immensely.

Also, don't be ashamed to take medication for crippling anxiety or debilitating depression. Make an appointment with your doctor to discuss whether it is right for you and to weigh the risks and benefits. Alternatively, I have personally found great improvement in my physical and mental health by working with a licensed dietitian, taking supplements, cleaning up my diet, moving my body, and living a healthier lifestyle.

I'm not qualified to share medical advice, but as your friend, I want to mention that it's worth focusing on your overall health and wellness because your body, brain, and heart are all interconnected. Grief, loss, and trauma impact them more than we realize, which is why I advocate for a holistic approach.

God has given us ways to heal physically, emotionally, and spiritually. I pray that the Lord will guide you on your healing journey and that when anxious thoughts cloud your mind, His light will shine in the darkness. In your own strength, you cannot control every circumstance or avoid every trigger. But with Jesus, you can face them all with His perfect peace.

PRAYERS TO HEAVEN

Jesus, our minds are anxious, and we often feel panicked. Every day, we encounter triggers that remind us of our baby and how deep our loss is. We are tempted to turn to worldly distractions to alleviate the pain. But You don't give as the world gives; You give us the best gift—Yourself. Thank You for Your Holy Spirit inside us to comfort us. Help us to protect our hearts while You heal us. Keep us grounded in You. Renew our minds and give us Your peace. Amen.

TRUTH TO CLING TO

Psalms 94:19; 121:1; Isaiah 40:31; 41:10; Matthew 6:34; Luke 12:22–34; 2 Timothy 1:7

TIME WITH JESUS

1. Which past, present, and future triggers do you struggle with? Inventory the places, people, or situations that impact you the most.
2. How can you protect your heart from these triggers? Write a list of boundaries you may need to set during this grief season.
3. Have you ever experienced amygdala hijack? Describe the situation and how you handled it. Then, write a plan for responding to your next moment of panic that includes a biblical grounding technique.

HEALING STEPS

1. Practice visual biblical imagery the next time you are anxious. Imagine Jesus sitting with you and holding you through it.

2. Memorize a comforting Bible verse. To help, download printable memory verse cards or buy Scripture memory temporary tattoos or stickers.

3. Listen to worship music and fully surrender to praising Him. I have compiled a playlist of my favorite worship songs for grieving and healing at BridgetsCradles.com /Worship.

4. If you need additional support, research and book an initial consultation with a Christian counselor, licensed dietitian, or doctor.

11

Holding Both

WHEN YOU EXPERIENCE BOTH
JOY AND SORROW

As sorrowful, yet always rejoicing.

2 Corinthians 6:10 ESV

Trigger Warning: pregnancy announcement, living children, rainbow babies

I closed myself into the seclusion of my closet, knowing a breakdown was upon me. I laid baby girl clothes that I had bought for Bridget six years earlier on the floor. I knelt in front of the pile and knew it was time—time to let myself grieve the fact that she never got to wear them, and I would probably never use them for a daughter on earth.

Tears cascaded down my cheeks as I picked up each one to ceremoniously say good-bye—not to the clothes but to the person I had hoped would wear them. Floral designs danced across their fabric in beautiful arrays of pinks and purples, patterns unfamiliar to me during the past three years of raising Bridget's little brother.

Oh, how badly my heart had longed to raise a daughter. I had dreamed of brushing her long brown hair, putting in pretty bows, and picking out matching outfits. I wanted to do all the girly things with her: playing with dolls, painting our nails, and making crafts and jewelry. But more than living out these childhood dreams, I had longed to raise a daughter into a godly woman. I wanted a close mother-daughter relationship for the rest of my life.

When Bridget died, I didn't just lose a baby. I lost the opportunity to see her grow up, graduate from high school, get her first job, meet her soulmate, and walk down the aisle. I lost the chance to be the grandmother to her children. People sometimes don't realize that when you lose a baby, you don't just lose them as a baby. You lose them as a child, teenager, and adult. You grieve an entire lifetime of hopes and dreams.

But what led me into the closet that day almost six years later? Honestly, it's a difficult story for me to share. I fear you might judge me the same way I judged myself. But I want to be transparent with you because it's the reason I learned the true meaning of *holding both*. I'm praying my vulnerability will help you *hold both*—sorrow and joy, grief and gratitude—in your circumstances too.

In June 2020, I was eight weeks pregnant with our third child. It had been almost six years since Bridget went to Heaven, and our toddler son had just turned three. We had been trying to get pregnant for nearly a year using the same fertility treatments that had helped us conceive our son. However, every month—after the dreaded two-week wait—we were disappointed to see only one line on the pregnancy test: not pregnant.

Then, I would bleed, and we would start the whole cycle over again. If you've struggled with infertility, you know what it's like to ride this exhausting emotional roller coaster. From tracking your cycle days, taking shots and medications, checking your cervical mucus, predicting fertile days, and timing everything perfectly, the process can be overwhelming and disheartening. There were times when I doubted if I would ever be able to conceive and carry a baby again. We were building a new house in hopes of growing our family. We had started trying to get pregnant long before the builders broke ground, hoping to bring a new baby with us when we moved in. But they poured the concrete foundation, and I wasn't pregnant. Then the framing went up, and I still wasn't pregnant.

In an act of faith, I wrote the name we had chosen for a baby girl on the wooden frame above the future nursery door. But even after they completed the sheetrocking, siding, roofing, plumbing, and electrical work, I still wasn't pregnant. The flooring, cabinets, trim, and hardware were installed, but still no double pink lines.

The night before we moved out of our old house, I wrote in my "one line a day" journal: "I feel my period coming. I am almost ready to give up. I have lost so much hope. Why won't my body conceive? I am so exhausted from this move."

The very next day, on the final day in our old house, God unexpectedly answered our prayers! I reluctantly took a pregnancy test and was stunned to see a faint double line. I wrote in my journal: "Wow! God, You shocked me with the most amazing gift and miracle! Thank You, Thank You! I can hardly believe it! You are so good and kind." What a difference a day makes!

I surprised Matt by holding up the pregnancy test stick when we took a final picture next to the "SOLD" sign in our front yard. In one photo, we captured the bittersweet emotion of leaving behind our first home together—the house where I was pregnant with Bridget, where Bridget's Cradles began, and where we brought home our first son and raised him for his first three years of life.

We were leaving behind many memories, yet we were excited to start our family's next chapter in our new home. We trusted

God's timing and knew this precious baby was worth the wait. Overjoyed and filled with gratitude, we thanked God for our little miracle.

I was sick during my first trimester and experienced many symptoms similar to my pregnancy with Bridget that I hadn't experienced during my pregnancy with my first son. Even the palm on my right hand was dry and peeling like it had been with her. I was convinced we were having a girl. The thought of finally decorating a girl's nursery filled my heart with excitement!

I couldn't wait to put floral wallpaper on the white walls of the room we had reserved for our new baby. I spent the first few weeks of my pregnancy daydreaming and revisiting my Baby Girl Nursery Pinterest board, which I had pinned for years, ever since I was pregnant with Bridget.

I was looking forward to having a baby shower for a girl, something I never got to do with Bridget. I started looking at invitations, decorations, and cake designs. In my typical fashion, I had it *all* planned out: a naked floral cake with pink and peach roses, gold accents, and tulle-wrapped balloons.

In hindsight, I shouldn't have let my heart get so carried away with desire, but I couldn't help how much I longed for a baby girl. We could hardly wait to confirm our baby's gender, so we took an early sneak peek gender test at eight weeks. A friend received the results by email and placed a box on our porch containing a onesie that revealed our baby's gender. Would it be pink or blue?

We waited to open the box until after our son went to bed. We stood in our bedroom, and my heart raced as I cut open the box, hoping to see a little pink onesie inside. But as soon as I glimpsed the blue, my heart sank, and I immediately ran out to our back deck to cry, too ashamed to let my husband see my true feelings.

Honestly, I feel embarrassed to share my reaction with you too. But in the moment, my heart needed to feel the weight of what it was feeling. I expressed my disappointment to God and let my tears fall one after another as I cried under the light of the moon. I went to bed hoping I would wake up the next morning feeling grateful and joyful for the gift of another sweet baby boy. However, I woke up still immersed in sadness. So I pulled Bridget's clothes from the storage bin in our basement and headed for the closet, leading us back to the story that opened this chapter. In being disappointed over not having another girl, I realized how much I was still grieving Bridget. Was the hope of *eventually* having a daughter a crutch I had been leaning on all these years?

Was it preventing me from grieving her fully? If so, the crutch had now been yanked out from beneath me, and I found myself limping without it. Conflicting emotions overwhelmed my heart: joy for a new life, disappointment over unmet desires, gratitude for the gift of a baby boy and younger brother for my older son, sadness over Bridget, and excitement for a future with two sons.

I hadn't seen my counselor in years, but I knew I needed to process this with her. I scheduled an appointment and arrived at her office a few days later, feeling slightly nervous. I feared she would judge me for how I was feeling—after all, I was a mom who lost a baby. Shouldn't I just be grateful to have a living baby regardless of their gender?

I sat on her comfortable couch and immediately felt at ease. I told her everything that led to my meltdown with Bridget's clothes in my closet: the year of infertility, building our house, moving in, finding out we were pregnant, hoping it was a girl, then learning it was another boy.

Before she could say anything, I quickly added, "I know I should be grateful to have a healthy baby, and I am. I feel bad for feeling this way. I really do love this baby boy. I'm excited for our older son to have a little brother. I believe God chose this boy for us, but I can't shake this feeling of sadness over not having a girl. It's making me miss Bridget so much."

I paused and took a deep breath, waiting for her response. With a loving tone and not a hint of judgment, she said, "Ashley, you know it's okay to *hold both*, right? It doesn't have to be either-or. You can be excited about this baby boy's life *and* disappointed you're not raising a daughter. You can be grateful *and* grieving."

Her words resonated deeply within my soul and permitted me to feel precisely what I was feeling—both! But why did my brain try to force me to feel one or the other? Logic told me both feelings couldn't be true simultaneously and that, somehow, the positive should override the negative. But here's what I've learned: A gift doesn't cancel out a grief.

• • • *And, Not But* • • •

We often minimize or justify our conflicting emotions using the conjunction *but*. For example, "I am grateful for my living children, *but* I'm missing my baby in Heaven." Instead, we should use the conjunction *and*, such as "I am grateful for my living children, *and* I miss my baby in Heaven." Both statements are true.

Having living children in your home doesn't nullify your grief for your baby in Heaven. Some of you may have lost a twin or baby in a pregnancy with multiples. At their delivery, you felt the tension of holding both as you said hello to one baby and good-bye to another. You continue to carry the weight as you raise your child without their sibling, every day a reminder of who they would have been.

What about you? Have you experienced any of the following examples of *holding both*?

- Feeling sad for yourself *and* excited for others?
- Being disappointed in your circumstances *and* thankful for the blessings God has given you?
- Experiencing pain *and* finding purpose in it?
- Grieving your baby in Heaven *and* wanting to have another baby?

- Feeling underlying sorrow *and* being able to have fun with your friends and family?

As grieving mothers, we feel guilty for smiling or laughing because our grief connects us to our babies. If we are not consumed by it, we worry we are not honoring them. We fear others may perceive a happy outward appearance as a sign that we are no longer grieving.

So we hold on to grief—and the appearance thereof—because it is an expression of our love. But this can make us apprehensive about returning to our normal lives. As a result, we avoid attending events such as weddings and going on vacations because we feel guilty for having fun. When around other people, we hold back our smiles and become anxious when they ask us how we are doing.

After Bridget went to Heaven, it was hard for me to engage in surface-level conversations and everyday social interactions. *No, I don't want to talk about the weather or my weekend plans. My baby just died!* It all felt so trivial. My advice to you when you are ready? Take the trip. Laugh at the joke. Smile. Just because you have a temporary moment of joy doesn't mean you don't miss your baby! Grief is all-consuming enough. We should welcome a reprieve from the relentless sadness when it comes.

Others don't see the whole picture of your grief. They don't see the tears you shed privately. They don't know what is best for you in your healing journey. Two months after Bridget died, Matt and I traveled to Europe with his family to tour Christmas markets in three countries. I was worried others would judge us for going on a trip so soon after her death. But escaping our daily life and getting away together was so healing for us.

My mom knit mint and lavender "prayer squares" for us to take with us (which we now call memory keepsakes, if you're familiar with our ministry). We took pictures with them as we stopped at many famous bridges in Budapest, Vienna, and Prague. At each bridge, we sprinkled dried lavender flowers into the river below, calling it "Bridges for Bridget." We were holding both. We missed her, *and* we went on a vacation. We honored her memory, *and* we enjoyed a trip together. *And*, not but.

• • • AM I REALLY HEALED? • • •

Our second son's gender reveal brought to the surface a wave of grief that had been building up inside me. Despite my happy life, there was a lingering sadness I had been suppressing. It was as if a dam had finally broken, and the floodgates of my sorrow could finally flow. Grieving like this years later made me question whether God had really healed my heart as much as I thought He had.

I was living a fulfilled life, raising my toddler son, serving in ministry, and expecting again. God had brought joy back to my life, and I was content and grateful. I had made significant progress in my walk with the Lord to the extent I was supporting other grieving moms on their own journeys.

Yet here I was on the closet floor, doubting if God had done a work in me. Why was I still so sad? Why wouldn't He fulfill my desire to raise a daughter on earth? I was back to square one with the *why* questions and doubting God's plan for me. My friend, have you been there too?

This is exactly where Satan wants to keep us: in a place of perpetual disappointment—the chasm between our expectations and reality. He wants us to believe God is purposely withholding something good from us. He wants us to think the story God is writing for us isn't a good one.

The enemy also tries to convince us we are not making progress in our spiritual growth. Experiencing intense

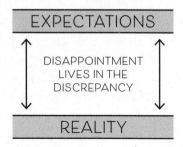

EXPECTATIONS

DISAPPOINTMENT
LIVES IN THE
DISCREPANCY

REALITY

emotions again is not an indication that God isn't healing you! Nor does it invalidate the healing that has already taken place. As we've learned, grieving is essential to the healing process. So if there's more grief, it means there is more healing work to do. Our hearts will always ache for our babies, and the healing journey will last a lifetime. Personally, I will miss Bridget for the rest of my life. I am certain her sweet face will be the last thing on my mind before I take my final breath, no matter how long I live.

Although God will restore joy and purpose to our lives on earth, our hearts won't be *fully* mended until we leave behind the brokenness of this world. The ultimate redemption will occur when we reach Heaven and are reunited with our precious children. There will be no need to *hold both* because we will be *holding them*. But earthside, how long until the all-consuming sadness subsides?

• • • TIME HEALS? • • •

The well-known phrase *time heals all wounds* implies emotional pain will eventually wane given enough time. However, I don't believe that time alone can heal the deep wound of losing a baby. Time on its own only takes you further from the moment you carried your baby.

If you incessantly dwell in sadness, the passing of time will keep you stuck in grief. The key to healing is Jesus, who transcends time and promises you a future with your baby. As the psalmist declared, "He heals the brokenhearted and binds up their wounds" (Psalm 147:3).

In fact, it is *by His wounds* that we are healed (1 Peter 2:24). If you remove Jesus from the equation, you are left with only grief and time. Gaping wounds left alone won't heal. We need Jesus to bind our wounds, and His process takes time.

Grief + Time ≠ Healing
Jesus + Grief + Time = Healing

Elisabeth Kübler-Ross is famous for exploring the five stages of grief: denial, anger, bargaining, depression, and acceptance. She studied these stages while researching patients who had received a terminal diagnosis. The stages reflect the emotional states the patients experienced while coming to terms with their impending death.

Some scholars believe that we go through similar sequential stages when grieving the loss of a loved one, but I disagree. Based on my personal experience, grief is not a linear process with clearly defined stages that we move through in a set order, never to return to previous stages.

I believe grief is more cyclical than linear. Jesus leads us through a process of grieving, healing, and then grieving again, which leads to even more healing. This cycle repeats itself until "He who began a good work in you" has carried it out to completion (Philippians 1:6).

In the months after Bridget's death, I was in survival mode. My emotions were all over the place. One moment, I was at peace, and the next, I was angry and questioning God. Then suddenly, I was sobbing uncontrollably, missing Bridget more than my heart could bear. There was no predicting my emotional state from day to day or even hour to hour.

As time went by and I believed I had reached the stage of acceptance, I would suddenly be overwhelmed by grief again. Significant milestones in my life would pull me back into the depths of my sorrow. Sometimes, even the tiniest triggers could evoke the strongest emotions. Grief is a complex process that cannot be neatly compartmentalized or contained. It is unpredictable and does not resolve quickly.

In today's fast-paced world, we are accustomed to our instant culture and expect to have everything now. The desire for instant gratification is hardwired within us and may tempt us to try to expedite our grief. Healing with Jesus takes time and cannot be fast-tracked. Time with Him allows perspectives to shift, hope to grow, and joy to be restored. There is a sanctification process that occurs in the messy middle of grief that cannot be rushed.

Jesus knows what He is doing and is intentional in how He heals us. He lets grief resurface because it exposes unhealed areas of our hearts and allows us to go deeper with Him. Jesus gently peels back each layer of grief and applies His salve at a pace we can handle. We should not compare our grief timetable to someone else's, even if they experienced a similar loss.

Each person grieves differently because we are all uniquely made by God, and our life stories are all different. Setting expectations for how long it will take to grieve will leave you disappointed. Give yourself grace if you are not where you think you should be, and know Jesus is going to heal you on your own timeline.

THE RAINBOW OF HOPE

It's human nature to want to tie up sad stories with a pretty bow. We all love happy endings and redemption stories! However, when it comes to pregnancy and infant loss, we need to determine what constitutes a happy ending. We might believe that having another baby, a *rainbow baby*,[1] will fill the void in our hearts for the baby we lost.

---

1. *Rainbow babies* is a term used for living babies born after the "storm" of pregnancy or infant loss.

But personally speaking, neither of my sons has replaced Bridget or made me miss her any less. While they have brought immense joy to my life, they have not filled the hole in my heart that aches solely for *her*. Jesus is the only One who can do that. Plus, what if I had not been able to have more children?

Our hope can't be contingent on our circumstances or expectations. Sadly, not everyone can have the desired number or gender of kids they had dreamed of. Babies cannot be where we place our hope, nor can they be the redemption plan for our loss—that is too big of a burden for a child to carry. The baby our hearts truly long for is the One who laid in a manger in Bethlehem over two thousand years ago. We hinge our hope on Jesus' birth, life, death, and Resurrection!

Our happy ending is not here on earth. It is in Heaven. Jesus is our redemption story. He is the One who has fixed the problem of death and will reunite us with our children. No matter what trials we face on this earth, we have a glorious future that awaits us in Heaven.

Is it wrong, then, to desire another baby and to want to raise children on earth to know the Lord? Absolutely not. These are good, godly desires. After all, God commanded us to be fruitful and multiply (Genesis 1:28). But we must be cautious not to turn babies into idols or let the pursuit of them overtake our identities.

Motherhood is one of God's greatest gifts. However, being a mom should not define our entire identity. Instead, God intends for us to find our identity in Him. First and foremost, we are followers of Christ. Being a mother is a *role* we have in fulfilling the Great Commission of making disciples. If God blesses us with rainbow babies, it is our responsibility to raise them to be followers of Jesus.

The rainbow biblically represents God's covenant with humanity, promising He would never flood the earth again (Genesis 9). After a storm, He displays His bow in the sky to remind us that He always keeps His promises. The rainbow of His faithfulness—rather than the rainbow baby—is the beautiful bow that wraps our stories in hope!

Note: Our second son, Brenner, was born in 2021. He is joy personified. I love him so much and wouldn't want him to be anyone other than who God made him to be: a little boy. I am incredibly grateful God blessed me with two sons. *And* I grieve the hopes and dreams I had for raising a daughter on earth. I have found contentment in knowing God gave me the children He intended for my family on earth. *And* I am excited to spend eternity with Bridget in Heaven. I am *holding both* and trusting God with my story.

Prayers to Heaven

Jesus, we struggle with feeling both sorrow and joy, grief and gratitude. Help us navigate these conflicting emotions and allow us to hold both. Give us patience to walk with You on this journey, knowing it takes time for You to heal us. Remind us that You're not withholding anything good from us. Remove disappointment from our hearts so that we can be content in the life story You're writing for us. Thank You for being the ultimate redemption in our stories and for giving us the rainbow as a sign of Your everlasting faithfulness! Amen.

Truth to Cling To

Psalm 30:2; Psalm 84:11; Ecclesiastes 3:4; Isaiah 53:4–5; Jeremiah 17:14; John 15:11; Romans 15:13

TIME WITH JESUS

1. What are some conflicting emotions you've experienced? Write down ways you are *holding both* using *and* statements instead of *but* statements.
2. The enemy wants you to believe Jesus isn't working in your life or healing your heart. Write a list of evidence to the contrary. In what ways have you witnessed and felt Jesus' healing touch?
3. Disappointment lives in the discrepancy between our expectations and reality. Fill out the chart in your *CIH Guided Journal* to process any feelings of disappointment you may have with the Lord.

HEALING STEPS

1. Have you built a dam to hold back the waters of your grief? Consider breaking it down to let your emotions flow. This release might be the breakthrough you need to move into the next chapter of your healing journey.
2. Healing with Jesus takes time. Reflect on the ways you may have been trying to rush the process. Commit to slowing down and being intentional about your time with Him.
3. After it rains, stand outside and look for a rainbow. Then, read Genesis 9 to be reminded of God's faithfulness to His promises.

12

More Than Gold

WHEN YOU ALLOW GOD TO TRANSFORM YOU

On that day you will be glad, even if you have to go through
many hard trials for a while. Your faith will be like gold that has
been tested in a fire. And these trials will prove that your faith
is worth much more than gold that can be destroyed. They will
show that you will be given praise and honor and glory when
Jesus Christ returns.

1 Peter 1:6–7 CEV

Trigger Warning: living children, medical trauma

I stared at my feet and the carpet pattern beneath them, my
body crouched over in disbelief. Sitting in a waiting room at a
children's hospital three hours from our home, my body threat-
ened to collapse under the weight it was carrying. My hands held
my head, and my elbows leaned on my knees for support. Tears

blurred my vision, and anxious thoughts swirled through my mind. *Was this really happening?*

Our two-year-old son was on the operating table, undergoing emergency surgery. At seven o'clock in the evening, we were the only ones in the waiting room. The quiet, empty room would be ours for the next three hours. A phone hung on the wall—it will ring, they told us, when they have an update. Until then, wait.

I went to the bathroom, certain I would vomit my heart right out of my chest. My baby boy was fighting for his life, and I couldn't do anything to help him. In the seclusion of the bathroom, I cried out desperately to the Lord, "Please don't take him! I need him here! Please, God, save him!" All my faith was in God and the surgeon, who happened to be the chief of pediatric surgeons, miraculously on call that night.

Earlier in the day, our son, who has severe food allergies and gastrointestinal issues, had undergone an outpatient GI procedure to dilate his pylorus, the opening from his stomach to his intestines. Three months before, he'd had this same procedure done at a children's hospital in another state, and it was successful in improving his symptoms of low appetite, poor weight gain, and difficulty eating a normal volume of food.

This time, we were at a different children's hospital with a different gastroenterologist. However, during the procedure, something went horribly wrong. While trying to dilate his pylorus, the doctor accidentally perforated it, which caused his stomach contents to leak into his abdominal cavity and turn his body septic.

Unaware of what had happened, the medical team discharged him from the hospital. We took him back to our rental home to let him nap so his anesthesia could wear off before our three-hour drive home. However, we knew something was not right as we tried to rock him to sleep. He started to vomit, and his face turned pale and his lips turned blue.

We immediately drove him to the emergency room at the same children's hospital. He lay on my chest, weak and unresponsive, as they took his vitals and labs. The room seemed to spin, with doctors in and out as I held my boy's nearly lifeless body. I looked at Matt and repeatedly said, "I'm terrified. I'm terrified." *What was happening to my baby boy? Was he going to be okay?*

They did a scan of his abdominal cavity and found air— meaning there was a hole in his GI tract. They rushed him into emergency surgery to repair it, triggering memories of the moment I was separated from Bridget in the hospital as I handed her over to the funeral home. I kissed him, and they wheeled him away, taking my heart with him.

After three agonizing hours, the phone on the wall rang. I picked it up. A nurse informed us that our son was out of surgery and the surgeon would update us in person. We waited anxiously until the doctor who saved our son's life walked in wearing blue scrubs and a surgical cap.

It felt like an out-of-body experience as he likened our son's condition to a gunshot wound to his stomach. He told us if we hadn't gotten him to the ER when we did, he could have died. I sat in shock at the severity of our situation, yet in awe at the divine intervention that had saved him.

Our son was hospitalized for the next seven days, recovering from surgery and relearning how to eat and walk. He had a drain tube and four laparoscopy holes in his abdomen, as well as a nasogastric (NG) tube in his nose. The only comfort he found was when his Mommy lay underneath him in his hospital bed, which I did for an entire week. I sacrificed my comfort for his, while pleading with the Lord to heal him.

I remembered the story of the woman in Matthew 9 who was healed because of her faith. She believed that if she could just touch Jesus' cloak, her bleeding condition would be cured. As I lay with my son's body on mine, I imagined reaching up to Heaven and grasping for the hem of His garment.

I knew the enemy wanted this traumatic event to be the ultimate blow to my faith—the final straw that made me turn my back on God. But I needed Him more than ever. I thought, *If the devil thinks this is going to be the trial that finally breaks my faith and takes me out, he's wrong.*

I posted daily updates on our son's condition. We received an outpouring of support and messages from friends, family, and even strangers. However, I noticed two recurring themes in people's comments: They didn't think I deserved to go through it, and they felt I had already been through enough in my life.

They knew I loved the Lord and served Him wholeheartedly in ministry. They knew I had lost Bridget, and those closest to me also knew I had walked through a life-shattering, heartbreaking trial *before* meeting Matt and losing Bridget.

So, how could it be that I was facing yet another traumatic event? It just didn't feel fair that one person could go through so many trials. Though my friends were rightly sad over our situation, I realized that their well-meaning comments contained theological inaccuracies:

Statement	Theological Inaccuracy
You don't deserve to go through this.	If you follow Jesus (or you're a good person), you will be blessed and not face trials. Christians don't deserve to suffer.
You've already gone through enough.	If you've already gone through something hard, you won't have to go through more hard things. There should be a cap on how much suffering one person can endure.

The first is based on the prosperity gospel fallacy, and the second is simply untrue. Jesus told us, "In this world, you will have trouble" (John 16:33). On our journey to Heaven, our lives will be filled with trials of all kinds, but Jesus reminded us in this same verse "to take heart" because He has "overcome the world."

Sadly, there's no limit to the number, frequency, or intensity of trials we may experience in a lifetime. My life is a testament to the fact that there's no quota on the amount of grief you're allowed to face. In fact, the month after I submitted this book's initial manuscript, I experienced one of the worst tragedies of my life.

On July 28, 2024, my dad was hit by a drunk driver in a hit-and-run while he was on a motorcycle ride. The driver left him in the road to die, paralyzed and in critical condition. A kind woman and her daughter stopped, called 911, and performed CPR. He was rushed to the hospital, where he lived for a week on life support.

Watching my precious daddy suffer in the hospital for that week was excruciatingly painful. It was pure torture and the worst kind of mental, emotional, and physical anguish you could imagine. On August 4, 2024, I held his hand as he took his last breaths, surrounded by his loving family.

As I write these words, my eyes are puffy from crying. Tear-soaked tissues surround where I'm sitting at my desk. Moments before I mustered the strength to get on my computer to type these edits, I was on the floor sobbing. Friend, I am in deep, deep grief. I'm here with you now, and I've been where you've been.

I hate that you are experiencing the loss of your baby! It is absolutely the worst. Losing a baby at any gestation is traumatic and painful. If you experienced an early first-trimester miscarriage, you might be tempted to minimize your loss and feel as though you don't have the right to grieve the same way as a mother who experienced a later-term stillbirth. Or maybe a mother who experienced stillbirth at twenty weeks doesn't feel it's the same as losing a baby at full term or after birth.

First, grief is grief. Though our types and timelines of loss differ, we don't need to compare them to each other. At the beginning of every Bridget's Cradles support group, we read something we call our Declaration of Faith. I want to share the first paragraph with you:

> We believe that life begins at conception. Some of us here may have lost our baby at eight weeks, others at 38 weeks, and some eight days or even months after birth. Though our type of loss and

our grief may not be exactly the same, we choose to unite in our common heartache and our shared hope. We believe each baby, regardless of his or her gestation, or time spent on earth, has an eternal soul that is saved by the grace of Jesus and lives forever in Heaven. All of us here have children in Heaven, and we all lost our hopes and dreams for our children's lives on earth.[1]

So here we are together—you, me, and sadly, countless other women who have suffered the loss of a baby and share in this mutual pain. But what if I told you that the trials you've walked through in the past have prepared you for this one? Furthermore, what if I told you that the grief you're experiencing right now will prepare you for a future trial?

This is because trials change us—rather, *Jesus* changes us *through* trials. Walking with Him through a major betrayal and loss in my mid-twenties was the training ground that strengthened my faith before Bridget was born into Heaven, leading me to a place of surrender that opened the door for a ministry to be born.

Grieving and healing with the Lord through her loss prepared me to face my son's health issues and unexpected surgery with grace and strength. The sum of these past trials (and my sanctification through them) has culminated in a deeper faith that will now help me as I walk through the unthinkable tragedy that took my dad's life.

Speaking of my dad, he was a genius at making elaborate spreadsheets. He had one for everything: finances, of course, but also sports championships, his favorite musicians, information about the Great Lakes, and even one called "Through Time," which tracked important milestones and details in our family's lives.

I get my organizational OCD tendencies from him. And as I reflect on my dad's use of spreadsheets throughout his life, it makes me ponder an interesting thought: When it comes to trials I have endured, I am tempted to list them in a *hypothetical* spreadsheet titled "Bad Things That Have Happened to Me" or "Things I Wish Never Happened."

I don't know about you, but sometimes I feel the need to "document" just how unfair I think my life has been. And if I'm being totally honest, there's a part of me that wants everyone else to see this spreadsheet. It's not that I need to throw myself a pity party; I just want to feel seen and validated in my suffering. I long for my pain to be acknowledged—for someone to say, "I see you. That must be so hard." Do you ever feel the same?

But what if our trials were meant to be listed in a different hypothetical spreadsheet? Perhaps "Hard Things I've Been Through That Have Strengthened My Faith," or "Trials That Have Made Me More Like Christ," or "Things I Wish Weren't Part of My Life but God Used for Good"? The amazing thing about Excel is that existing cells can be moved over to a new spreadsheet. The same is true in life: We can choose to see our trials differently by adjusting our outlook. I'll show you how in this chapter.

• • • SPIRITUAL GROWTH • • •

In my mid-twenties, I sat in my pastor's office, trying to hold back the tears as he counseled me through the worst rejection and betrayal of my life. Years before I met Matt and we lost Bridget, someone I deeply loved and trusted deceived me and broke their promises to me. My heart felt as though it was irreparably broken, and I wondered how I would ever recover from the palpable pain I was in.

The trajectory of my entire life had changed, and my soul felt shattered. My pastor remained calm and attempted to infuse biblical hope into my weak spiritual veins. He grabbed a marker and started drawing a horizontal line sloping upward on a whiteboard. I watched him, not realizing that what he was about to say would stick with me for the rest of my life.

As he sketched the line, he made some small loops at the beginning, a big loop in the middle, and a few other loops toward the end, ending with an arrow pointing upward. He marked three *X*'s on the line: (1) right *before* the big loop, (2) in the *middle* of the big loop, and (3) right *after* the big loop.

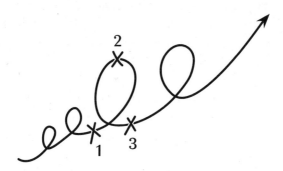

He pointed to the big loop and said, "The loops represent trials. This is the one you're in right now." He then pointed to each *X* and proclaimed, "Everyone on earth is either about to enter a trial (*X* #1), is in the middle of a trial (*X* #2), or coming out of a trial (*X* #3). And no matter where they are, they've already been through trials, and more trials are coming in their future."

Upon hearing that depressing statement, I quickly asserted, "*This* is all I can handle! There couldn't be anything worse than this. I can't imagine going through anything beyond this!" At the time, I thought the heart-wrenching relational trial I was facing was the worst thing that could ever happen to me. Little did I know that many more devastating "loops" were coming, and sadly, there would be much more than *this*.

Just a few years later, after marrying Matt and conceiving Bridget on our honeymoon, we were in our local hospital holding her tiny, lifeless body in a cradle. Nine years after that, we found ourselves in yet another hospital with our youngest son for emergency surgery on his stomach. A year after that, we were back in the same hospital Bridget was born in, but in the trauma unit, watching my dad suffer and die at the hands of a drunk driver.

The point my pastor was trying to make with his drawing: There will be trials! Each trial is an opportunity to grow in spiritual maturity and become more like Christ. When new challenges arise, you will reflect on God's faithfulness and trust that just as He helped you through the last trial, He will also help you through the current one. You may even embrace the trials, knowing they will ultimately work for your good.

The first big loop I encountered—the betrayal I faced years before Bridget was conceived—played a role in the creation of Bridget's Cradles. This particular trial in my life also grieved my mom as she struggled to watch me, her daughter, endure such incredible pain. The person who hurt me had also deeply hurt her. As a result of this trial, at twenty-five years old, I had to make a cross-country move back into my parents' house for a few months.

I was in such despair I could hardly eat or sleep. There were many days my mom physically fed me, and many nights she lay with me and tickled my back to help me fall asleep. To cope with her own grief, she learned how to knit. If it weren't for that season, Bridget's Cradles never would have existed because my mom did not know how to knit before that. Do you see how each loop influences the subsequent ones? In the next trial, we are not the same as we were before.

For example, after our son's surgery, he struggled for months with vomiting and unwanted GI symptoms. As his parents, we wrestled with the fear of the unknown. Would he ever get better? How would we help him now that we couldn't do the dilation procedure? To this day, we are still in the middle of this trial, struggling to feed him and help him gain weight.

He is still on a very restricted diet due to multiple food allergies, which stem from his diagnosis of food protein-induced enterocolitis. Every week, I take him to feeding therapy with a speech-language pathologist. This is hard stuff. Yet, I have noticed a shift in my outlook through this life trial compared with previous ones.

I don't feel the need to rush through it because I can see how God is shaping me in the middle of it. Something has changed in me. Brenner's feeding challenges have grown me in patience, gratitude, and steadfastness. This is now part of my testimony and will also be a part of his testimony.

My perspective of my circumstances and the types of questions I ask God in trials has changed over time. In the past, it was common for me to ask questions rooted in flawed theology (left side in the chart below). Now (most of the time), I ask questions that focus on God's redemptive character (right side):

Spiritual Immaturity (Our Human/Flesh Reaction)	Spiritual Growth (The Holy Spirit's Response)
• Why me, Lord?	• Why did You choose me for this?
• Why are You allowing this to happen?	• What do You want to teach me in this season?
	• What do I need to learn about You?
• What did I do to deserve this?	• What area of my life or heart needs pruning?
• Are You punishing me?	• What good will You bring from this?
• Where are You, God?	• Who do You want me to become through this?
• Why have You forsaken me?	• Who can I bless or comfort because this is now part of my testimony?
• How could You, God?	

I qualified with "most of the time" because I want to be fully honest with you. God has grown me spiritually over the years, but at the end of the day, I am still human. My knee-jerk response to new, painful trials often boomerangs back to the *why* questions—to question God for allowing more pain into my life.

My flesh's natural reaction is to leverage whatever control *I think* I have to wiggle my way out of the unwanted circumstance—or at least to get through it as quickly as possible. But Jesus gently reminds me, "There's something for you here. I'm here with you. I will get you through this, but don't rush past what I have for you in this season."

The Holy Spirit responds by prompting us to ask questions that lead to spiritual growth and a deeper trust in Him. Our holiness is shaped in the humility of our hardships. If only we would sit in them long enough for Jesus to transform us through them. So, my friend, can you embrace the hard but holy work He is doing in you right now?

• • • THE HARD BUT HOLY HARVEST • • •

In God's economy, suffering is valued, not because He enjoys watching us suffer but because it prunes us to bear more fruit for His Kingdom. The process of becoming more like Christ is called *sanctification*, and it involves the work of the Holy Spirit (1 Peter 1:2). None of us would have ever chosen to lose a child, but what if the harvest from our grief was so beautiful and bountiful that we became grateful for it?

In a parable, Jesus explained that He is the Vine, and His Father is the Gardener (John 15). We are His branches. He prunes the branches that don't bear fruit, but He also prunes the fruitful branches to bear even more fruit. Jesus emphasized we can only bear fruit if we remain in Him. If we are not in Him, we are "like a branch that is thrown away and withers; such branches are picked up, thrown into the fire and burned" (John 15:6).

My friend, your pain doesn't have to be in vain. You couldn't control your circumstances, but you now have the power to choose what to do about them. Don't throw away your branches. Don't waste your pain. Allow God to prune you so you can bear fruit. Why? According to Jesus, the purpose of producing fruit is to bring glory to the Father and to show that we are His disciples (John 15:8).

This is hard but holy work. It costs us! Jesus said that to be His disciples, we must deny ourselves, take up our cross, and follow Him (Matthew 16:24). Sanctification requires sacrifice and surrender. We need to let the Gardener do His work.

Although pruning is a painful process, we must remember that the Gardener:

1) Knows what He is doing.
2) Loves us.
3) Works for our good and His glory.

What does this mean for grieving moms? While sanctification is a part of *every* believer's journey, the loss of a child puts us in a unique position to experience intense spiritual growth. Our grief is so profound that it allows Jesus to radically transform us. In our brokenness, He can mend and mold our hearts to mirror His. As Isaiah beautifully expressed, "We are the clay, you are the potter; we are all the work of your hand" (64:8).

Grief is an invitation to intimacy with Jesus, an opportunity to know Him like you never have before. In your darkest moments, you will discover who He is and learn to rely on Him for your every need. Your desperation and despair will lead you to a deep dependence on your Savior.

My love for Jesus has grown the most during the hardest seasons of my life. When I had nothing left, He became my everything. When I was weak, He was my strength (2 Corinthians 12:9). I learned to trust Him in the valleys, not the mountaintops, for it is in these valleys "your faith will be like gold that has been tested in a fire" (1 Peter 1:7 CEV).

When life goes our way, we tend to forget about Him and live as if we don't need Him. But in the valley of the shadow of death? Oh, Lord, we need You. Every moment, we need You. His rod and staff comfort us (Psalm 23:4). He guides our steps and carries us when we are too weak to walk. He will lead us *out* of the valley, but we don't want to miss what He has for us *in* it. The valley is where sacred sanctification happens—where He sows seeds that will become a garden for His glory.

• • • GLORY AND SUFFERING • • •

We let Christ sanctify us so that He can give us a "crown of beauty instead of ashes," as described in Isaiah 61:3. This verse refers to God replacing the ashes on our forehead (an Old Testament symbol of repentance, grief, and death) with a beautiful garland on our head.

The Hebrew word for beauty, פְּאֵר (pǝ-'êr), translates to an embellishment or headdress. This was later translated into the English word *crown*. In Greek, the word δόξαν (*dóxa*) is used instead of *beauty*, and it means glory and honor. The same Greek word is used in 1 Peter 1:7 when Peter declares that the testing of our faith is worth more than gold because it results in "praise, glory, and honor when Jesus Christ is revealed."

Do you see this theme running across the pages of Scripture? Both the Old and New Testaments show a clear correlation between our present suffering and future glory. Read the following words of encouragement from Peter and Paul (emphasis added):

- "Dear friends, do not be surprised at the fiery ordeal that has come on you to test you, as though something strange were happening to you. But rejoice inasmuch as you participate in the **sufferings** of Christ, so that you may be overjoyed when his **glory** is revealed" (1 Peter 4:12–13).

- "The God of all grace, who called you to his eternal **glory** in Christ, after you have **suffered** a little while, will himself restore you and make you strong, firm and steadfast" (1 Peter 5:10).

- "If indeed we share in his **sufferings** in order that we may also share in his **glory**" (Romans 8:17).

- "Not only so, but we also **glory** in our **sufferings**, because we know that **suffering** produces perseverance; perseverance, character; and character, hope" (Romans 5:3–4).

Based on these verses, we can infer that suffering is valuable both for us and for God. It is something we should consider an honor to endure. As we miss our babies, we share in His sufferings. Remember, God Himself is a grieving parent. He watched His one and only Son die on the cross. As moms who have lost children, we can empathize with His heart in ways others cannot. Our grief gives Him glory!

But how? Peter gave us the answer: "So then, those who *suffer* according to God's will should commit themselves to their faithful Creator and *continue to do good*" (1 Peter 4:19, emphasis added). Remember the branches? Pruning them prepares them to bear fruit. Similarly, we are sanctified so that we will produce good works. He prunes us to prepare us for His purposes! Therefore, sanctification is the process through which God works *in* us so that He can work *through* us.

BEING SANCTIFIED
THROUGH SUFFERING

(A WORK IN US)

USING GRIEF
FOR GOOD

(A WORK THROUGH US)

• • • HEAVENLY TREASURE • • •

Why should we work for the Lord? Because "faith by itself, if it does not have works, is dead" (James 2:17 NKJV). This does not mean we need to earn our salvation with works. No, we are already saved by His grace. But if we love Jesus, we will desire to serve Him.

Our work for the Lord flows as an outpouring of His work in our hearts, compelling us to serve Him with our hands. We are filled with gratitude for His grace and want to share with others the hope we found in Him. Paul expressed that working for the Lord is our greatest calling and blessing (emphasis added):

- "Therefore, my dear brothers and sisters, stand firm. Let nothing move you. Always give yourselves fully to the *work of the Lord*, because you know that your labor in the Lord is not in vain" (1 Corinthians 15:58).

- "Whatever you do, work at it with all your heart, as *working for the Lord*, not for human masters, since you know that you will receive an *inheritance* from the Lord as a *reward*. It is the Lord Christ you are serving" (Colossians 3:23–24).

I have volunteered unpaid as the full-time executive director of Bridget's Cradles for the past ten years. Many people are surprised I have not earned any money for the countless hours I've given the nonprofit organization over the last decade.

Though I may earn a salary one day, serving in this ministry has never been about the money. Matt and I believe our family's financial sacrifice has been worth the Kingdom work we are doing. Every dollar donated is poured into our programs and services, allowing our ministry to grow and reach thousands of grieving families nationwide with the comfort of a cradle and the hope of the Gospel.

When people are stunned that I work full-time for free and ask why, I say, "I don't make dollars. I'm earning a better currency, a Heavenly one." This isn't just a witty comeback; I genuinely believe it. Heavenly rewards are eternal, unlike earthly riches, which do not last forever (Proverbs 27:24). We can't take our money or possessions with us when we die. All of it will fade away—the perfect house, the fancy car, the nice clothes, and all the *things* we think we need.

I'm not immune to our culture's obsession with *always wanting more—bigger, nicer, better.* My sinful heart is attracted to what the world has to offer, but Christ in me longs for eternal things. Jesus told us, "Do not store up for yourselves treasures on earth, where moths and vermin destroy, and where thieves break in and steal" (Matthew 6:19). Instead, He encouraged us to store up treasures in Heaven (v. 20).

Believers can earn five different crowns in Heaven for their service to Christ. I've summarized them in appendix 4, if you want to learn more about them. Paul told Timothy to command those "rich in this present age" not to put their hope in wealth (1 Timothy 6:17). He urged Timothy to remind them to instead do good, be rich in good deeds, and be generous and willing to share (v. 18). "In this way they will lay up treasure for themselves as a firm foundation for the coming age," he concluded in verse 19.

I'm not advocating that everyone quit their jobs and do unpaid ministry work (but if you decide to, I know of a good organization looking for volunteers). Half-jokes aside, I love Jesus' words in Matthew 6:21: "For where your treasure is, there your heart will be also." When we focus on the Kingdom, our hearts become interwoven with its King—the one who is and was and is to come (Revelation 1:8).

Friend, the loss of your baby most likely wasn't your first trial, and it won't be your last. But as you allow Jesus to sanctify you through your loops, you will one day help others through theirs. Your misery will be your ministry, your very life your mission field. Your "light and momentary troubles" are achieving for you "an eternal glory that far outweighs them all" (2 Corinthians 4:17).

One day, you will walk with Jesus on streets of pure gold on the New Earth. When you see the splendor of what God created out of your heartache, you will rejoice that you suffered for the sake of it. All the pain and trials you experienced living on a sin-soaked earth will fade into distant memories. As you hold your baby in Heaven, in the presence of Jesus, you will know your faith—tested through trials—was worth more than gold (Revelation 21:21; 1 Peter 1:7).

PRAYERS TO HEAVEN

Jesus, thank You for walking with us in the valley. Though it's painful, prune us so that we can bear fruit for Your Kingdom. Sanctify us and develop a deep spiritual maturity in us. We don't want our pain to be in vain. Use our suffering for Your purposes and glory. We long to serve You out of gratitude for all You've done for us. Remind us that our faith is worth more than gold. Bring a harvest from the hard but holy work You are doing in us. Amen.

TRUTH TO CLING TO

Luke 22:42; John 17:17; Romans 8:28; Romans 12:1; 1 Corinthians 6:11; Galatians 2:20; 1 Thessalonians 5:23

TIME WITH JESUS

1. Look at the chart on page 206 and consider the questions you're asking God during your grief. If you're asking questions on the left side, try asking the ones on the right. Use your *CIH Guided Journal* for this exercise.
2. What areas of your life need pruning? How do you see Jesus sanctifying you through this season? Surrender your heart to His hard but holy work.
3. Faith without works is dead. What is God putting on your heart to do for Him?
4. Read appendix 4, "Crowns in Heaven," on page 259. What crowns do you hope to receive in Heaven?

HEALING STEPS

1. Print our "Suffering and Glory" Bible memory cards from your *CIH Guided Journal*. Place them on your nightstand and read them each night before you go to bed.

2. Remember: God is with you when you walk through the valley of the shadow of death. His love will follow you all the days of your life. Commit Psalm 23 to memory. Listen to the *Cradled in Hope* podcast, episode 59, "My Shepherd in the Valley: Psalm 23."

3. Read the book of 1 Peter, which is the inspiration behind this chapter's title and content. It's only five chapters long and is one of my favorite books in the Bible. Peter's words are pure gold—pun intended—and contain so much truth, wisdom, and hope.

13

With the Same Comfort

WHEN YOU WANT TO USE
YOUR GRIEF FOR GOOD

> Blessed be the God and Father of our Lord Jesus Christ, the Father of mercies and God of all comfort, who comforts us in all our affliction, so that we may be able to comfort those who are in any affliction, with the comfort with which we ourselves are comforted by God.
>
> 2 Corinthians 1:3–4 ESV

Trigger Warning: funeral, burial

Five days after Bridget's birth // On October 27, 2014, our families gathered for a private service to remember Bridget. We set up tables in the church sanctuary near the altar with mementos from her life, including a teddy bear with her recorded heartbeat, baby shoes and onesies we had bought, and books we planned to read to her. The church staff illuminated the background walls with her mint green and lavender nursery colors and placed her tiny white casket next to a beautiful floral arrangement.

I wore a pink chevron dress, the same one I had worn at her gender reveal party just weeks earlier. I cut out a heart-shaped piece of fabric from inside it and placed it inside her casket to symbolize our mommy-daughter connection. We baptized her with holy water and sang "Jesus Loves Me."[1]

The pastor who had married her daddy and me performed her funeral. We celebrated her life, mourned her loss, kissed her good-bye, and wept many tears. We placed letters and special items inside her casket. Then, the funeral home director sealed it and drove her to the cemetery for her burial.

I'll never forget following the hearse from the church to the cemetery. It was one of the most surreal moments of my life. I remember thinking: *Is this really happening? Will I wake up from this nightmare?* As my mind struggled to grasp my current reality, I gazed at the overcast sky along our route.

Gray clouds blanketed overhead, mirroring the sadness in my soul. However, as we turned south, I noticed sunlight piercing through the clouds above the cemetery. I took a photo to capture God's grace in the moment. He knew my heart needed a ray of hope to get me through what we were about to do next.

I peered down into the rectangular hole in the ground where my daughter would be buried. After we said a prayer, my husband placed her casket in the grave. Then he shoveled fresh dirt over it until a mound formed above the earth, marking the spot where our daughter's body would one day be resurrected.

I couldn't bear to dwell on the six feet of physical separation now between us. Yes, Bridget's body was underground, but her soul was in Heaven. So I chose to focus on the latter, knowing I would be reunited with her one day. Our families then released

---

1. Bridget's baptism was a ceremony we decided to perform, but one not necessary for her salvation.

twenty-four balloons, one for each week I had carried Bridget on earth.

As the mint and lavender balloons drifted off in the gray sky toward Heaven, Jesus reminded me that He was with me and my daughter too. This wasn't the end of our story. As I reflected on my bed-rest declaration that nothing good would ever come from this, I felt Him stirring something new in my soul: *Maybe something good would come from this.*

Little did I know that, just moments before, our funeral procession had driven by the location of Bridget's Cradles' future headquarters. Though our future landlord wouldn't break ground on the Little Blue Barn until the following year, on the day of Bridget's funeral, we followed the hearse to her grave, passing by the land that would one day house her ministry.

We didn't use that highway often back then. But nowadays, I use it daily to drive between our headquarters and our new home, which we built near Bridget's cemetery. Every day on my short commute, I am reminded that God always has a plan to bring light from darkness. Through sunbeams shining on a cemetery, He gave me a glimpse of the good that was coming. Sweet friend, I pray you see that good is coming for you too.

◦ ◦ ◦ HOLY GRAIL OF GRIEF ◦ ◦ ◦

Where does the aspiration come from to see something beautiful resurrect from the ashes of our grief? God intricately wired us with an innate desire to restore things to His original design. As C.S. Lewis articulated in *Mere Christianity*, "If I find in myself a desire which no experience in this world can satisfy, the most probable explanation is that I was made for another world."[1]

As future citizens of Heaven, we can sense that this world is not what God created it to be. Losing a baby was not part of God's perfect design. Though we are confident God will eventually restore His creation, we long for things to be made right in the here and now. When we encounter a disparity between how things are and how they should be, we yearn for justice.

But finding purpose in your pain can feel like an overwhelming quest for the holy grail of grief. It may seem like you must attain it in order to validate your baby's life or vindicate their loss. But I want to assure you that you don't have to earn your way to Heaven to see your baby again. You don't need to be productive to bring worth to your baby's life. Release yourself from that pressure.

Our babies don't need us to do things for them because they are already blissfully experiencing the peace and joy of Heaven. They lack nothing and are fully satisfied in Christ. God assigned your baby's worth at conception and sealed their salvation on the cross. Both their life and yours have already been redeemed by Christ's death and resurrection for eternity.

Even though I have seen incredible good come from my daughter's life through her ministry and in my own life, I still have not been able to tip the scales of my suffering, so to speak. If my motivation was to outweigh the magnitude of my loss—Bridget's life—with good deeds, I would never be able to overcome the imbalance. Her life was too valuable, and I could never do enough to express my love for her.

Similarly, we could never earn our salvation from Jesus. We are saved by grace, through faith, not by works (Ephesians 2:8–9). There is nothing you need to do to earn the love of God or to justify the value of your baby's life. No amount of striving could ever balance the weight of your sorrows.

So, do I contradict myself when I encourage you to use your grief for good? No, because it's the *why* behind finding purpose in your pain that matters. There are two driving forces that will motivate you to serve others in memory of your baby:

1. a desire to honor your baby and leave a legacy for them
2. gratitude for your salvation and your devotion to following Jesus

When you love Him with all your heart, soul, strength, and mind (Luke 10:27), your heart breaks for what breaks His, and you long to build His Kingdom by sharing the Gospel. When I started Bridget's Cradles, some assumed it would be a temporary "grief project." They thought it would eventually fizzle out, and I'd move on to something else. If my motivation for leading the ministry was solely to satisfy my grief, they would have been right. However, I'm serving in the ministry to fulfill my life's purpose: to share the Gospel and make disciples.

Right after Bridget died, I never would have thought I would start a nonprofit, host a podcast, or write a book. I hadn't set out to do all these things and never would have imagined all this could come from my seemingly small acts of obedience over time. I am just a small-town girl from Kansas. If God can do it through me, He can do it through you too. He can do *anything* through you if it is His will and you give Him your surrendered heart.

But God can't give you an assignment if your hands are tightly clenched around your own plans. You may have to let go of something in order for Him to give you something better. This can be hard, but I encourage you to open your hands and make room for what the Lord has for you.

Each of you will have a different assignment than I do, and that's a good thing. In 1 Corinthians 12, Paul likened the Church to the Body of Christ. He used this metaphor to remind believers that they are *all* important members of the body, each with unique gifts. God created us with specific strengths, passions, talents, and skills that He wants to use for His purposes. You fulfill your calling by using the gifts He's given you for His glory.

Five months after Bridget's birth // We converted Bridget's empty nursery into an office. I started designing the Bridget's Cradles website on my laptop while my mom knit more cradles for our local hospital. I had gone back to work as a speech-language pathologist but focused on forming the ministry during my nights and weekends.

One day, while walking our golden retriever, I asked God, *What do You want from me? What's the end goal of Bridget's Cradles? Should our cradles be in every US hospital?* Out in an open Kansas field, I heard Him reply, *"I want every grieving family to know Me and to spend eternity with their baby in Heaven."* His profound response would become our ministry's mission statement: "We provide Christ-centered comfort, hope, and healing to families grieving the loss of a baby in Heaven."

The following month, a local news station featured us, and the story ended up airing nationwide. Suddenly, hospitals across the country were requesting cradles from us, and knitters and crocheters were signing up to volunteer. We hired a lawyer, became an official 501(c)(3) nonprofit, and set up our post office box. Soon after, I resigned from my career to lead Bridget's Cradles full-time.

• • • OUR GREATEST PURPOSE • • •

Discovering your purpose can feel daunting, but I think we often overcomplicate it. As believers, we all have the same simple purpose: to love God and love others (Matthew 22:36–40). The Great Commission, found in Matthew 28:19, outlines our primary duty: to make disciples of all nations and baptize them in His name.

Jesus' followers are called to make disciples who make disciples (2 Timothy 2:2). Once we have been saved and understand the depths of His love, why wouldn't we want to share the hope of our salvation with those who don't know Him?

If you are on a quest for the elusive holy grail of grief, I can point you in the right direction: You will find purpose in your pain when you encounter Jesus. *He* is your ultimate purpose. If you pursue purpose solely to fulfill an inner need or to alleviate your grief, you will miss it! By serving the Lord Jesus Christ, you will discover your life's true purpose.

What is the difference between *purpose* and *calling?* Your purpose is the overarching reason for your existence. It remains the same in and out of seasons of grief—to share the Good News of Jesus. However, your calling is how you live out that purpose, and it is tailored to how God made you and what interests you. It is more specific and personalized to you, based on your experience, expertise, and talents.

Now that you've lost a baby, you may be wondering, *What's my calling now?* If we were talking as friends over lunch, I'd ask you, "What are you good at? What breaks your heart?" Lean into your strengths and passions. Spend time in prayer, asking the Lord for direction. Read His Word, and most importantly, wait on Him. He will be faithful in revealing what He wants you to do in His perfect timing.

I have witnessed firsthand how God can use a mother's grief for good. Here are some examples from moms who have attended our support groups:

Grieving Mom *In Memory Of*	Calling
Casey *Son Jack Monroe*	Serves weekly at Bridget's Cradles; does Random Acts of Kindness (RAK) on her son's Heaven Day
Brooke *Daughter Georgia Grace*	Started a balloon business and blesses grieving families with her decorations at Bridget's Cradles special events
Jennifer *Daughter Talia*	Pumped breast milk after her daughter was stillborn and donated over 20,000 ounces to more than twenty babies in need
Rebekah *Daughters Eliana & Annalynn*	Started a pregnancy loss support group in her town and volunteers at her local pregnancy resource center; recorded a video of her story and shares her testimony at churches
Annie *Son Parker*	Called hospitals on behalf of Bridget's Cradles and facilitated sending thousands of cradles to grieving families

continued

Grieving Mom *In Memory Of*	Calling
Sara *Sons Charlie, Cooper, and Camden*	Delivered cradles to hospitals in her home state and coordinated a hospital visit with Bridget's Cradles when I was in town; won our Shine Their Light award during our annual Wave of Light fundraiser by raising the most funds in memory of her three sons
Maria *Daughter Taylor*	Creates beautiful social media graphics for our podcast *Cradled in Hope* to encourage grieving moms with quotes and Scripture

Do you see how each mother's calling is different, yet their purpose—to glorify God in their grief—is the same? My friend Kelcey serves at our headquarters every week in memory of her son, David, who was stillborn at seventeen weeks. After holding him in one of our blue cradles at the hospital, she wanted other grieving families to be comforted by a cradle. She said, "If David were here, I would spend my time with him. Since he's not, I'm spending this time serving others in his memory."

Her profound statement made me think, *What if our motherhood for our babies in Heaven looked like serving others on earth?* Healing happens when we "get outside our grief" and shift our focus to others rather than solely looking inward. Our local support group is named Support and Serve. We start with prayer, worship, a biblical message, and small group discussion similar to traditional support groups. But we end with a time of serving, using our hands to comfort others.

When mothers leave our support groups, they drive away from the Little Blue Barn knowing the cradle they tagged or the hospital box they packed will comfort a family who has experienced the same pain they have. This is fulfilling Paul's command to comfort others with the same comfort we have received from God (2 Corinthians 1:3–4).

Five years after Bridget's birth // On a random Saturday, I was driving on the highway I mentioned earlier when a large "FOR

RENT" banner in front of a little blue barn caught my eye. God stirred my spirit, and I immediately took the next exit and called the number listed. To my surprise, the landlord answered and offered to show me the property right away.

Within minutes, I entered the empty room and was taken aback when I saw the back walls were already painted mint green, the color of Bridget's original cradle, and also the branding of our ministry. Months later, we moved the ministry out of our home and cut mint and lavender ribbons to celebrate the grand opening of our new headquarters.

• • • SMALL BEGINNINGS • • •

I frequently give tours of our "one-room HQ" in the Little Blue Barn, where we run our ministry operations. When visitors see the floor-to-ceiling racks of cradles for babies born into Heaven, they are amazed by the impact that comes from such a small space in little Kechi, Kansas.

At the time of this writing, we are currently donating cradles to over 1,500 hospitals in all fifty states and have donated over 250,000 cradles and memory keepsakes since we started the organization.[2] When I tell visitors this fact, they usually respond, "Wow, I can't believe you did all of this!" To which I always say, "I didn't do this. It was God." They smile, then say, "Yes, it was God, but you were clearly a part of it." And I respond, "He needs faithful servants to carry out His work."

Friend, extraordinary things don't usually happen overnight. When Bridget's Cradles first started, we served only a few local hospitals. We often worried we wouldn't have enough cradles to supply their needs. I would reach into near-empty bins in Bridget's nursery, our first headquarters, and pray a volunteer would send more soon so we could fulfill the next hospital order.

---

2. These numbers will be outdated soon after the date of this printing, as Bridget's Cradles sends cradles to new hospitals each week.

Almost a decade later, we now receive hundreds of boxes of cradles made by our nationwide team of knitting and crocheting volunteers. Annually, we send over 30,000 cradles and memory keepsakes to hospitals to comfort grieving families. How did we get here? It all began with a surrendered "yes." Then, it was sustained by thousands of small "yeses"—each an act of obedience, day after day, week after week, year after year.

My advice to you: Just get started. Though moving past the starting line may feel insignificant, it's often the hardest step to take. The enemy will attempt to thwart you from being obedient by placing fears and doubts in your mind. I love what Zechariah said when he prophesied about building the second temple: "Do not despise these *small beginnings*, for the Lord rejoices *to see the work begin*" (Zechariah 4:10 NLT, emphasis added).

We want to be women of faith who take action and start the work, knowing our Father will rejoice over our small steps of obedience. You don't have to do something grand to bring God glory. It can be as simple as talking with someone, taking them out to lunch, or sending them some encouraging text messages.

You could volunteer at your church or favorite ministry or donate to a nonprofit in memory of your baby. Each time you share the hope of Christ, you are planting a seed for His Kingdom. Don't underestimate the significance of sharing your story. Besides your salvation, it may be the most important thing you possess. We triumph over the enemy by the *word of our testimony* (Revelation 12:11).

Sister, your testimony is more powerful than you realize. Because you've lost a baby, you now have the opportunity to witness to people you wouldn't have been able to reach before. While imprisoned, Paul wrote to the Philippians, saying, "I want you to know, brothers, that what has happened to me has really served to advance the gospel" (1:12 ESV). During his time in chains, he ministered to the whole imperial guard!

God had a plan for Paul's captivity, and Paul acknowledged that his imprisonment was "for Christ" (Philippians 1:13 ESV). His prison cell turned into his pulpit.[2] What if you viewed the loss of your baby in the same way? What if losing a baby has really served to advance the Gospel, and your grief is for Christ?

As a grieving mom, it may feel like all eyes are on you as people watch how you will cope with this tragic event in your life. You didn't choose this spotlight, but you now have a platform to share the hope you've found in Jesus. Perhaps there's a family member who doesn't believe in God, a friend struggling with her faith, or even a stranger who could be impacted by your story. What if the Lord uses your testimony to bring them to Christ?

People relate to us in our weakness. Our testimony becomes stronger through our suffering. Vulnerability encourages vulnerability. People open up to us when we open up to them. We build trust with others by sharing the deepest, most painful parts of our lives. In doing so, we open the door to reach their heart with the Gospel.

So wake up each morning and say yes to what He asks and no to what He doesn't. Serve Him by serving others. Share your baby's story and your testimony in Jesus Christ. Be obedient in planting the seeds even if you don't know if someone's heart soil is ready to accept them. If they're not open to following Jesus now, He could tuck your testimony in their heart to be used later in their lives. He will water your seeds and bring them to harvest in His timing.

We are called to obedience, not the outcome. God is responsible for what He will do with your acts of service. You may never know what will come from the seeds you plant this side of Heaven. I'll never get to meet every mom who received one of our cradles, listened to our podcast, or even read this book. Still, I plant, knowing I'll see the harvest in Heaven.

You may never see the big picture or the final result. Don't let it prevent you from moving forward. The Lord will direct your steps and lead you. Though you may have a vision for what you hope to accomplish, your story is the Lord's to write. You are the pen; He is the Author.

• • • FOR THE ONE • • •

We often use a phrase at Bridget's Cradles: "Do it for *the one*." If you visit our headquarters, you will see bins of cradles from floor to ceiling. Our volunteers process hundreds of incoming cradles from our knitting and crocheting volunteers, and then hundreds of cradles are shipped back out to hospitals each week.

In a sea of thousands of cradles, it would be easy to overlook each one that was lovingly created for a family to hold their precious baby. We never want to lose sight of the person behind the numbers: the volunteer, the family, the baby. As we pack hospital boxes, we believe God already knows the name of each baby who will be held in our cradles.

We share families' stories in our monthly volunteer newsletter to help our volunteers feel personally connected to the grieving families they lovingly serve. It's important for them to hear directly from those who have received their cradles—providing powerful reminders that each stitch is made for "the one."

Last year, we organized a material drive to collect needed supplies, such as ribbon spools and crosses, to adorn our cradles. Someone hand-delivered two small bags of charms, each containing 100 crosses, and said to me, "I know it's not much, but I wanted to do something."

Since every cradle from Bridget's Cradles has a small cross charm affixed to the end, I responded, "For 200 families, this will be the cross on their baby's cradle. You have no idea how much this will mean to them." No, our hope is not in a cross charm; it's not even in a cradle. Our cradles only provide temporary comfort, but Jesus offers eternal comfort.

Detached from the Gospel, our ministry would be devoid of true hope. So whatever you do, big or small, do it for "The One"—Jesus Christ. He is the only One who can offer genuine comfort and everlasting life. Anything you do on this earth apart from Christ will fade away, but anything you do for Him will last forever. Your obedience and availability are all He needs to work through you for His Kingdom. As you take one small step after another, the days will turn to weeks, weeks to months, and months to years. Slowly, over time, you will see He is growing something beautiful in and through you.

Ten years after Bridget's birth // I am writing the final words of this book at my desk in the Little Blue Barn. I am listening to piano hymns as a candle softly glows next to my computer. Two purple cradles—which are the perfect height and softness—prop up my wrists, tired and trembling from all the hours of typing.

I glance out the window to see cars passing on the highway that Bridget's hearse once drove on. As I reflect on all that has happened—and will continue to happen—within these walls, I realize I am on sacred ground. It is here that thousands of precious cradles are sewn, carefully packaged, and sent to hospitals for grieving families nationwide.

Here we host volunteer gatherings, record podcasts, and link arms with grieving moms in our support groups. In this small building in Kechi, the Gospel is going forth to the nations. I hear the Lord gently say to me, "Nothing good will ever come from this? Oh, My daughter, just you wait and see . . ." //

I'm burning my seventh candle since I started writing this book, and it's on its last bit of wax. In a way, it's symbolic of where I'm at as I close these final chapters. When this candle burns out, I'll light another one. And even when I finish this book, there will be more for me to do. As long as I have breath in my lungs, I will keep shining my light for Christ.

In Matthew 5, Jesus told us we are "the light of the world," and we should let our light shine before men so "that they may see your good deeds and glorify your Father in heaven" (vv. 14–16). My mission is not yet complete. I am still running my race for Christ. And so are you, my friend. Jesus has a mission for you. Keep running! Light another candle and shine His light. Work for the Lord until you see Him and your baby face-to-face.

Prayers to Heaven

Jesus, we surrender our suffering to You. Use every tear we've cried for Your glory. We don't want our heartache to be wasted. Show us how to use our giftings and grief for good. Provide clarity on our calling as we fulfill our purpose to make disciples in Your name. Help us take the first step, knowing You rejoice over small beginnings. Keep us focused on serving "the one" who needs to hear about You! Let us see the beauty that comes from our small acts of obedience. We trust in Your timing and plans. Amen.

Truth to Cling To

1 Corinthians 9:24; 2 Corinthians 4:7–9; Philippians 2:13; Philippians 4:13; Hebrews 12:1–3; Hebrews 13:20–21; 1 Peter 2:9

TIME WITH JESUS

1. Do you feel pressure to find purpose in your pain? Release these feelings to the Lord and write a prayer surrendering your suffering to Him, opening your palms to receive His plans.
2. What do you dream of doing for God's Kingdom? Use the chart in your *CIH Guided Journal* to help you discover your calling.
3. The Lord rejoices in seeing the work begin. What is holding you back from getting started? Reflect on any fears, doubts, insecurities, or confusion you may have. What will help you confront these obstacles?

HEALING STEPS

1. Sometimes, God uses other believers to give us clarity on our calling. Talk with a trusted friend and brainstorm ways the Lord could use your giftings and grief for good.
2. Get started. Even if it's a small act, the Lord will be delighted with your obedience. Send the text. Make the call. Share your story. Write the post. Volunteer. Donate. Do a random act of kindness (RAK). Take the next step!

    ✐ We have RAK ideas and cards you can personalize in memory of your baby at BridgetsCradles.com/RAK.
3. Who is "the one" person God has placed on your heart to share His hope with? Pray for them, then serve them in some way: Write a card, bring a meal, give a thoughtful gift, or simply spend time with them.

14

Our Future Forever

WHEN YOU LONG FOR YOUR HEAVENLY HOME

> My Father's house has many rooms; if that were not so, would
> I have told you that I am going there to prepare a place for you?
> And if I go and prepare a place for you, I will come back and take
> you to be with me that you also may be where I am.
>
> John 14:2-3

I remember the day Bridget went to Heaven as if it had happened just yesterday. It's been ten years, but the memory of being in that hospital bed, holding her inside the cradle my mom had knit for her, is still vivid in my mind.

I gazed at her in awe, trying to memorize her face and preserve every detail. Aware of the transient nature of time, I forced my brain to capture mental photographs. I gently kissed her nose and lips, closed my eyes, and attempted to freeze time. I didn't want to forget the feeling of her skin against mine. These moments were fleeting, and I was determined to etch them into my memory forever.

A decade later, I can still clearly recall the sensation of her flesh and the features of her face. Yet other days, it feels like an infinite chasm divides the only time I had with her from the time that keeps ticking now. Can you resonate with this feeling? Whether you carried your baby for seven weeks or seven months or they lived for seven days, the time disappeared too quickly.

Oh, how we wish we could go back in time to be pregnant with them again or hold them one more time! We just want *more:* more moments, more memories, more time with them. We weren't ready to say good-bye! And though the day of their death was officially the day we "lost" them, each day that passes without them feels as if we are losing them all over again—because we expected them to still be in our lives today.

Time feels so elusive, always slipping through our hands. As grieving moms, we understand more than anyone else just how short life can be. James, Jesus' half brother, also recognized the fleeting nature of life when he remarked, "For what is your life? It is but a *vapor* that appears for a little time and afterward vanishes away" (James 4:14 RGT, emphasis added).

In our support groups, I use a skein of yarn—a staple in our ministry—to illustrate this concept to grieving moms. I unwind the yarn, pass it around the circle, and say, "What if this yarn had no ending? Imagine it just kept going and going! Across our state, then across the country, over the ocean, to other countries, and back and forth to us without end."

As they attempt to grasp the idea of a piece of yarn that never ends, I bring their attention to a small section in my hand. I say, "If the never-ending yarn represents eternity, then this tiny section represents the history of humankind on earth. And this"—pointing the tip of my fingernail inside the section—"would represent *your* time on earth. And an even smaller speck inside that, which is hardly visible, would be your baby's life."

This illustration may initially make you feel sad, thinking your baby's life—or even your own life—is somehow insignificant due to its brevity. However, it's important to remember we are eternal beings, and our worth is not measured by the length of time we live on earth but by the One who created us.

While visiting Bridget's grave one sunny afternoon, it occurred to me that unless the Resurrection happens in my lifetime, friends and family will eventually come to the same cemetery to visit *my* grave. It was a sobering thought that reminded me of my own mortality.

As morbid as this may sound, I then lay down in a field of open plots across from Bridget's grave and imagined that one day my body would be six feet under the ground. I squinted my eyes as the sun shone brightly above me and watched the clouds float by in the sky. The thought of death used to disturb me, but I felt an overwhelming peace that day as I daydreamed about being in Heaven with my daughter.

In chapter 7 we learned that our bodies are simply the earthly tents that house our eternal souls and spirits. When we die, we leave our mortal body behind, but our immortal spirit will live *somewhere* for eternity. Except for believers who are alive at the Resurrection, we must all experience a physical "first death." This is the only death followers of Christ will experience. Those who do not accept Jesus as their Savior will face the "second death," which is an eternity in the Lake of Fire (Revelation 21:8).

Did you catch that? *Not everyone* will die the first death (1 Corinthians 15:51). One generation of believers will not have to experience physical death! How is this possible? Paul referred to this coming Resurrection as a "mystery." Some Christians, including myself, believe the Resurrection will occur at the Rapture of the Church, before Jesus' Second Coming.

Others believe it will happen in one simultaneous event at His Second Coming. What matters most is that believers in Christ are assured to be with Him forever—either at their own death or at the Resurrection, whichever happens first. If you've never studied the End Times before (known as *eschatology*), it's important to understand that these viewpoints are *not* central to the core doctrine of Christianity.

They are not a salvation issue; therefore, Christians can hold differing views without compromising their unity in the body of Christ. We can all agree that at some point in the future, Jesus will resurrect us, and we will live on the New Earth with Him forever. Whether it happens in our lifetime or not, this Resurrection is the pinnacle moment when Jesus will reunite us with our babies in the flesh!

Paul described this moment in 1 Corinthians 15 and in 1 and 2 Thessalonians. He said that *not all people* will die but will be changed "in a flash, in the twinkling of an eye" (1 Corinthians 15:52). At the sound of the last trumpet, Jesus will raise the "dead in Christ" first, and then those "who are still alive" will be "caught up together with them in the clouds to meet the Lord in the air" (1 Thessalonians 4:16–17).

If this event occurs while we are still alive, Jesus will first empty the graves of our babies (and all believers in Christ who have died) and give them their glorified bodies. Even if we chose cremation for our babies or never received their remains, Jesus will make them whole again. Then, we believers who are alive will meet them in the air, and Jesus will also give us our glorified bodies. But what if this doesn't happen during our lifetime?

In that case, the Resurrection will be the moment when Jesus gives us *and* our babies immortal bodies at the same time (since we both would be considered the "dead in Christ"). If we die before the Resurrection, our soul would immediately be in the presence of our baby's soul in the temporary Heaven, but we would still be waiting for the Resurrection of our bodies. At the sound of the last trumpet, our souls will be united with our glorified bodies—at the same moment our babies' souls are united with theirs.

• • • HOMESICK FOR HEAVEN • • •

I've had many conversations with grieving mothers who have expressed a desire to be with their baby in Heaven. They are not suicidal, but they long to be reunited with their precious child. Although it may seem contradictory to long for Heaven without wanting to die, I believe it's not only possible, but biblical, to feel this way.

According to the Bible, we are "temporary residents" of this earth, merely "passing through" (1 Chronicles 29:15 CJB). The NIV translation of this same verse refers to us as "foreigners and strangers" of this world. Paul wrote that "our citizenship is in heaven" because we "eagerly await a Savior from there" (Philippians 3:20).

This world is not our permanent home. We can feel it deep within our souls. This homesick feeling is eloquently expressed as "longing for a better country—a heavenly one" in Hebrews 11:16. And Paul reassured us that our eternal Home is in Heaven: "For we know that if the tent that is our earthly home is destroyed, we have a building from God, a house not made with hands, eternal in the heavens" (2 Corinthians 5:1 ESV).

Therefore, he urged us to set our minds "on things above, not on things on the earth" (Colossians 3:2 NKJV). We have a glorious future filled with eternal joy that awaits us. Instead of fixating on what is behind us, we should focus on what is to come. I love these comforting words spoken by Jesus: "Now is your time of grief, but I will see you again and you will rejoice, and no one will take away your joy" (John 16:22).

Read those red-letter words again: No one will take away your joy. Oh, this promise hits deep with me. I know you feel it too, momma. Right now, your joy is gone. The brokenness of this world has worn you down, and the enemy has stolen so much from you. But to think that one day you will be joyous in the presence of Jesus, and no one—and nothing—will be able to take it away.

Can you imagine a place without sin and death? There will be no hospitals in Heaven. No ambulances or ERs. There will be no diagnoses, disabilities, illnesses, or infections. There will be no morgues, funeral homes, or cemeteries in Heaven. We will never again attend a memorial service or burial.

We will never see another casket, grave, or headstone. We will never have to read or write an obituary ever again. We will *finally* say good-bye to death and every awful memory associated with it forever. All of these "former things" will have passed away (Revelation 21:4 ESV). Does this sound too good to be true? In the very next verse, John said, "Write this down, for these words are trustworthy and true" (Revelation 21:5).

• • • THE PROMISE OF PROPHECY • • •

We live in a unique period in human history, between Jesus' First and Second Coming. Living after Jesus made His ultimate sacrifice for us on the cross is a tremendous blessing. We no longer have to offer animal sacrifices for our sins, as our ancestors did under the Law of the Old Covenant.

When we put our faith in Jesus, He remembers our sins no more (Hebrews 8:12). However, we still live in this broken world and are currently separated from our children. Remember the "already but not yet" of chapter 7? We are redeemed but not yet fully restored or resurrected. For this reason, I believe our broken hearts will not be *fully* healed until we are with our babies and loved ones in Christ again.

When we closed Bridget's casket for the final time, a sinking sadness came over me as I realized I wouldn't see her sweet face again until Heaven. I couldn't fathom waiting an entire lifetime for that moment. I pictured myself old and gray on my deathbed, taking my final breaths as visions of her turned from earthly imaginations into a Heavenly reality.

Oh, what a beautiful day that will be! But it feels too far away. Though I am not guaranteed to live another day, if I were to live to a hundred, I would have to wait over half a century to see my daughter again. Maybe you've thought about this too. But here's where we come back to the hope of the coming Resurrection and Jesus' return. We *might not* have to die a mortal death or wait an entire lifetime to see our babies again!

In our current time, we are witnessing what many believe to be the fulfillment of the signs of the End Times as prophesied by Jesus. These signs include wars, rumors of wars, earthquakes, famines, and pestilences. Jesus foretold these signs to His disciples on the Mount of Olives in the week leading up to His crucifixion. These teachings are known as the Olivet Discourse and can be found in Matthew 24, Mark 13, and Luke 21.

Based on the numerous prophecies in the Bible, including the Olivet Discourse and those centered around the nation of Israel, it is likely we could witness Jesus' return in our lifetime! Yes, I *genuinely* believe we could be alive for Jesus' Second Coming, meaning that we could be *currently* living in biblical times.

I understand that some people may scoff at this possibility, but in reality, it only fulfills prophecy. Peter told us that in the last days, scoffers will say, "Where is the promise of His coming?" (2 Peter 3:3–4 ESV). Friend, He is coming back, and He is coming back soon. God has given us a detailed playbook of what's to come in His Word. Revelation is the only book in the Bible that promises a blessing to those who read it (Revelation 1:3).

I can personally attest to that fact. Reading Revelation has been a great source of encouragement in my walk with Christ, especially as a grieving mother. As I look forward to seeing Bridget again, studying prophecy has further fueled my hope. Did you know that over a third of the Bible contains prophecy? From Genesis to Revelation, all the pages of the Bible point to a Savior, one who would come a first time and then a second time.

In fact, the first prophecy of Jesus occurs in the Garden of Eden after Adam and Eve sinned. God declared to the serpent (the devil), "I will put enmity between you and the woman, and between your offspring and hers; he will crush your head, and you will strike his heel" (Genesis 3:15). This verse is the first reference to a coming Messiah and is often called the *protoevangelium* or "first gospel."[1] A few verses later, God provides Adam and Eve with the first animal sacrifice, "garments of skin," to clothe them (Genesis 3:21).

Many of the prophecies—written hundreds of years before Jesus' birth—were fulfilled in His first coming, such as His birth in Bethlehem (Micah 5:2), His riding on a donkey into Jerusalem (Zechariah 9:9), and His hands and feet being pierced by crucifixion (Psalm 22:16). However, there still are prophecies in the Bible that have yet to be fulfilled, many of them reserved for the End Times, culminating in Jesus' Second Coming.

Why am I so eager to share this with you? Because there are no other prophecies that need to be fulfilled before the Resurrection occurs, which I believe will happen at the Rapture of the Church.[1*] Our "blessed hope" (Titus 2:13) is imminent! For grieving mothers, the Resurrection will fulfill our greatest desire—to be with our babies again *in the flesh.*

Can you imagine the reunion? I want you to think about it. I mean, *truly* let your heart and mind envision it. It's not wishful thinking, friend. It's really going to happen. Your faith will become sight, and your eyes will gaze upon your child's face. Your hands will hold theirs. You will hug and kiss them. And so you will be together forever.

Now, in full disclosure, I am skipping over some key periods in the timeline of the End Times, such as the Seven-Year Tribulation and the Millennium (Christ's thousand-year reign).

---

1. Based on a pretribulation, premillennial, dispensational eschatology viewpoint and timeline. The author acknowledges that there are other viewpoints.

However, a full teaching on eschatology is outside the scope of this book (and I also recognize there are differing beliefs on the chronology of the timeline, so I have chosen to focus on the bigger picture).

Friend, the promise of prophecy is this: God is faithful. He has carried out His Word and kept His covenant with His people. Our Heavenly Father sent His Son, Jesus, to be our Savior, just as He said He would. We have the cradle in Bethlehem and the cross at Golgotha to prove that He is a promise-keeping God. So when He says He will split the sky and return for us, we should believe Him (Revelation 6:14).

Throughout Scripture, God reminds us repeatedly that Jesus is coming back to earth (Matthew 25:31; Hebrews 9:28; Revelation 1:7, to name only a few). After Jesus ascended into Heaven, two men dressed in white[2]* told His disciples that Jesus would return from Heaven the same way they saw Him go, which was in a cloud (Acts 1:9–11).

Because God has always been faithful to His Word, we can trust that Jesus' Second Coming is a guaranteed promise that will surely be fulfilled exactly as He said. The most beautiful part of prophecy is that we already know how the story ends! We have a wonderful, hope-filled future that awaits us once Jesus destroys death and God throws Satan into the Lake of Fire forever (1 Corinthians 15:26; Revelation 20:10).

The present Heavens and earth will melt by fire, and the holy city, the New Jerusalem, will come down from Heaven to the New Earth. This will be our forever Home where we will live with God Himself in a perfect Paradise, Eden restored (see Revelation 20–22).

---

2. Scripture does not explicitly say who these two men were. Some theologians believe they were Moses and Elijah (based on the account in Luke 9:29–30), while others surmise they could have been angels.

• • • KEEP YOUR LAMPS BURNING • • •

So what should we do while we wait for Jesus to return? Jesus Himself told us to occupy the time and continue to do business until He comes back (Luke 19:13). He said, "Stay dressed for action and keep your lamps burning, and be like men who are waiting for their master to come home from the wedding feast, so that they may open the door to him at once when he comes and knocks. Blessed are those servants whom the master finds awake when he comes" (Luke 12:35–37 ESV).

What does it mean for us to keep our lamps burning? It means we shine the light of Jesus in this dark world. We keep working, serving, loving, growing, and building the Kingdom. We stay alert, watchful, and ready. In 2 Thessalonians 3, Paul warned believers against idleness and encouraged them to "never tire of doing what is good" (v. 13).

In many ways, Bridget's death woke me up from my slumber of lukewarm Christianity. Her life ignited a fire in me to urgently spread the Gospel. Knowing my days are limited, I now want to use each one of them for His glory. The reality is that there will soon come a day when our opportunity to reach people for Christ will be forever lost. There will be no need to evangelize in Heaven. The time is now to share the hope of Jesus with a lost and hurting world.

As Christian parents, our ultimate aspiration is to raise our children to know the Lord and join us in Heaven. I take comfort in knowing one of my three children is already there. Bridget's salvation is secure, and now Matt and I have the sacred responsibility of leading her two younger brothers to Christ so that our family can *all* be together in Heaven one day.

King Solomon, renowned for his wisdom, said children are a heritage from the Lord, like arrows in the hand of a warrior. He proclaimed, "Blessed is the man who fills his quiver with them" (Psalm 127:3–5 ESV). Even though Solomon was most likely referring to living children, I believe our babies in Heaven should still be considered arrows in our quiver. They should not be considered a *loss* for our family but a *gain*. Their brief lives on earth allowed us to gain eternal members of our Kingdom family.

Though our earthly family may not look as we had hoped, and one or more of our children may be missing from our family photos, we can rest assured that one day, Jesus will make our families whole. In the meantime, our babies in Heaven can still tremendously impact this world.

Think about your baby and the lives he or she has touched or changed, including your own. Has your baby brought you closer to Christ? Was your baby's life a part of someone else's salvation decision? Just think—there are babies in Heaven whose lives have spurred their parents and others to believe in Jesus!

Can you imagine a greater purpose our babies could have than winning souls for Him? Their lives bear witness to the Good News of the Gospel. We are their earthly counterparts, now entrusted with carrying out their legacy for Christ. As Matt and I serve in Bridget's memory, we want our ministry to reflect Matthew 6:10 (emphasis added): "Your kingdom come, Your will be done, *on earth as it is in Heaven.*"

Bridget's Cradles has two sides: one in Heaven, where Bridget resides, and one on earth, where we serve Jesus in her memory. We are in this together, even though we currently live apart. One day, God will roll the sky back, and Heaven and earth will become one! We will walk on the New Earth with our Kingdom family and never be separated again.

In the meantime, we have work to do (and there's work God is doing *within* us). He has a good plan for you, even if your life story isn't going the way you wanted it to. I know this feeling because my life has been *far* from what I had hoped or expected it to be. In the last twelve years, I have faced more trials than most people do in a lifetime.

If I could have been the author of my own story, I definitely would have written it differently! I would have omitted the tragic parts and left out all the sadness, grief, and loss. However, when I envision my final destination in Heaven and look at my life through the lens of eternity, I have a different view of my earthly trials. Oddly, I have an appreciation and respect for the journey that has made me who I am today.

The painful pressing has shaped me into Christ's likeness—a process of sanctification that I'm still undergoing and that won't be fully complete until I'm in Heaven. Without my suffering and surrender, He wouldn't have been able to use me for His purposes. Bridget's Cradles wouldn't exist, nor would this book.

My friend, what is it for you? What wouldn't have existed without your suffering? Maybe it's a change of heart, a newfound compassion for others, a ministry, or a closer relationship with Christ. Maybe it's a new hobby or friendship, a restored marriage, or a different path in life. Or maybe you're still waiting to see it come to fruition. Let me encourage you that God is always working behind the scenes.

I love the New Living Translation version of 2 Corinthians 12:9 (emphasis added): "My grace is *all* you need. My power works *best* in weakness." You don't have to be strong, feel all the way healed, or be "put together" to serve Him. Jesus' power works best in your weakness—yes, even through your tears, doubts, questions, and insecurities.

All He needs is your heart, and all you need is His grace. Even if it feels like all you can muster is a dim light, a flicker of a flame in the night, just keep your lamp burning. Shine the light of Jesus in the darkness of your grief as you eagerly await His return.

• • • ONE DAY CLOSER • • •

When I think of the story of Lazarus, I often resonate with Mary's honest reaction to Jesus when He came four days *after* her brother had died: "Lord, if you had been here, my brother would not have died" (John 11:32). I don't know about you, but I've often cried out a similar lament: "Lord, if You had done something, Bridget wouldn't have died."

Jesus, if only You would have *been there*, right now my baby would be in my belly / cradled in my arms / taking their first steps / going to kindergarten / graduating from high school / fill in the blank for your situation. But what we forget is that earlier in the story Jesus had been made aware that Lazarus was sick. He knew His friend was going to die, and yet He delayed His travel. Why? He said, "It is for God's glory, so that God's Son may be glorified through it" (John 11:4 ESV).

Although Jesus knew He was going to raise Lazarus back to life, He still wept over His friend's death when He encountered Mary and Martha on His way to Bethany. The two words *Jesus wept* are some of the most powerful in the Bible. First, we see that Jesus wept over death, meaning it deeply grieved Him (even though He holds power over it). Second, we see Jesus' humanity and compassion for us in His tears.

But I want to step back and focus on Martha's initial reaction to Jesus (prior to Mary's response). She said, "Lord, if you had been here, my brother would not have died. But I know that even now God will give you whatever you ask" (John 11:21). To which Jesus replied, "Your brother will rise again" (John 11:23).

At this point in the story, Martha assumed Jesus was talking about the "resurrection at the last day," which we've been talking about in this chapter. But little did she know that He was about to empty Lazarus's tomb and raise him back to life that very day. The previous four days she had spent grieving, she didn't realize that Jesus was on His way, and He was bringing with Him His Resurrection power.

This is an incredible story that should give us much hope. Though I wish Jesus was presently walking the earth and could visit our babies' graves *right now*, I want you to know something very important: He is on His way! And He is bringing His Resurrection power with Him because that's who He is: He is "the resurrection and the life" (John 11:25).

Though we have to wait longer than Mary and Martha did, we can be assured that Jesus is coming. He hasn't forgotten about us or our babies. Their graves and urns will one day be as empty as the tomb Jesus left three days after being killed on a cross. My friend, the Resurrection changes everything. Your precious babies will be raised to life. What more, as grieving mothers, could we possibly hope for?

But how long must we wait? Let's go back to the early days of the Church when the majority of the New Testament was being written. At that time, Jesus' disciples were fervently expecting His return, believing it could happen within their own lifetimes. When greeting or parting ways, the Jews would use the word *Maranatha*, an "Aramaic term that means 'the Lord is coming' or 'come, O Lord.'"[2]

But here we are, over two thousand years later, and we are still anxiously waiting for Jesus to return. Because it's been so long, our generation has lost the sense of imminence surrounding His Second Coming. Many have forgotten or seem apathetic that He could return any day now.

While it's true that no one knows the day or hour He will return (not even Jesus Himself or the angels—only God the Father), nonetheless, Jesus told us we should keep watch and be ready "because the Son of Man will come at an hour when you do not expect Him" (Matthew 24:36–44).

I love the poignant lyrics from the hymn "It Is Well with My Soul," penned by Horatio Spafford in 1873. His words beautifully encapsulate the longing and anticipation we should hold for Christ's return:

> But Lord, 'tis for Thee, for Thy coming we wait,
> The sky, not the grave, is our goal;

Oh, trump of the angel! Oh, voice of the Lord!
Blessed hope, blessed rest of my soul!

And Lord, haste the day when the faith shall be sight,
The clouds be rolled back as a scroll;
The trump shall resound, and the Lord shall descend,
Even so, it is well with my soul.[3]

What makes these lyrics even more powerful is that Horatio wrote them while on a ship passing over the waters where all four of his daughters drowned in a shipwreck.[4] Before that tragedy, he had lost most of his wealth in the great Chicago fire of 1871; he also later lost his young son to scarlet fever.[5]

After enduring such hardships, Horatio wrote that he had "peace like a river" as he looked out over the deadly sea and declared, "It is well with my soul." It's hard to believe he could feel this way after experiencing such horrific nightmares. The only explanation is that Horatio experienced Jesus' peace that surpasses all understanding (Philippians 4:7).

Despite losing children in tragic ways, Horatio anchored his hope in Christ. He chose not to look back on the trauma he experienced on earth but instead to look forward to when he would be with his children again in Heaven. The sky, not the grave, is our goal!

As time continues to quickly pass since the last day you carried your baby in your womb or held them in your arms, it may feel as though you are traveling further and further away from them. But I want to remind you of an important truth: Each day further from their death is one day closer to being with them again—whether in the clouds at the Resurrection or at your final breath—whichever comes first. Charles Spurgeon said, "The best moment of a Christian's life is his last one, because it is the one that is nearest heaven."[6]

For followers of Jesus, death is our birth into forever. Ten years after Bridget's death, I am focused on looking forward to the thousands and thousands of years I'll spend with her in Heaven rather than looking back on the short amount of time I had with her on earth. I am waiting every day with eager hope, excited for Jesus to take me Home to her.

Sweet mommas, we are so close; Heaven is near! The sky will be rolled back as a scroll, and every eye will see Him (Isaiah 34:4; Revelation 6:14; Revelation 1:7). Soon, we will be homesick no longer. This is why I love studying prophecy in God's Word. Though some use it as a scare tactic to warn us of the world's apocalyptic end, God gave it to us so that we could rejoice in our glorious future with Him.

In fact, the final verses of 1 Thessalonians 4, which discuss the Resurrection, end with "Therefore *encourage* one another with these words" (v. 18, emphasis added). As the world gets darker and we approach His Second Coming, we can be confident that our future in Heaven will be bright. This is because, for Christians, the end is really just the beginning of our future forever.

So, sister in Christ, look up. Jesus is on His way! Your reunion with your precious baby is near. Your story isn't over. Soon you will suffer no more, and Jesus will wipe away every tear you've cried. You will trade your suffering for glory and wear crowns of beauty for eternity with your son or daughter.

So take heart. Don't grow weary in doing good. You are one day closer! His Kingdom is coming. Soon, and very soon, you will be Home with your baby. Hold on just a little bit longer.

Maranatha. He is coming soon!

PRAYERS TO HEAVEN

Jesus, we can't wait for You to reunite us with our babies. Thank You for giving us the blessed hope to spend eternity with our Kingdom family. Fix our eyes on the glorious future that awaits us. *Remind us that we are citizens of Heaven, merely passing through this earth on our way to You. Let us boldly and urgently proclaim Your Gospel until You take us Home or You return, whichever happens first. Maranatha, oh, Lord, come. We long to be with You in our Heavenly Home. All glory to You forever. Amen.*

TRUTH TO CLING TO

Isaiah 11:1–9; 65:17–24; Zechariah 14:9–11; Daniel 12:1–2; Mark 13:24–27; Luke 10:20; Revelation 21:3–5

TIME WITH JESUS

1. Have you thought about your own mortality? Do you long for your Heavenly Home? Imagine your future reunion with your baby and write down how you envision it.

2. How can you "occupy the time" as you wait for Jesus to come back? What does "keep your lamps burning" mean to you?

3. Revisit the Hope Statements you wrote in your *CIH Guided Journal* during the introduction, "Hugs at the Door." I asked you to imagine what it would look like if Jesus healed your heart. Now that we've taken this journey together, how many of your Hope Statements have come true? Reflect on the work the Lord has done in and through you as you've read this book.

HEALING STEPS

1. If you want to learn more about Bible prophecy, I've compiled a list of my favorite books and resources on my blog. But first and foremost, I suggest you study the Bible itself, starting with Daniel and Revelation. I promise you will be blessed.

2. Listen to "It Is Well with My Soul." Think about Horatio Spafford's faith in the midst of his circumstances as you sing the words.

3. Write the word *Maranatha* somewhere you will see it every day. Each time you do, pray to the Lord as you long for His return.

Parting Words

Sweet sister,

You did it. You read this entire book! I know it must have taken so much strength to keep picking it up and pressing into your pain. I am so proud of you, and I can only imagine how far you have come. It was a true honor for me to walk with you and hold your hand through it.

I'll be honest: I don't like good-byes. I've never been good at them. If you live in the Midwest, like I do in Kansas, you're probably familiar with what we call a "long good-bye." It usually goes like this: After spending hours chatting with a friend while sitting on their couch, you finally get up to leave.

The two of you stand by the front door, chatting for another fifteen minutes and hugging good-bye several times, yet you keep finding just one more topic to discuss. Eventually, someone reaches for the door, but the conversation doesn't end there. Your friend walks you to your car, and you continue talking in the driveway for another thirty minutes before finally saying good-bye.

I've had many of these long good-byes standing outside the Little Blue Barn in Kechi, hugging grieving mommas and sharing as many comforting words as I can before it gets too late, and they need to head home. In a way, the end of this book feels like that—like you and I are standing out by your car, and I don't want our conversation to end.

However, I've run out of word count, and I must give you one final hug and send you on your way. But this is not good-bye! It's a "See you later," and "I hope our paths will cross at some point" (perhaps in our Cradled in Hope Facebook group or online support group, Hope Online).

Your healing journey doesn't end here, but I hope my words have pointed you in the right direction—toward Jesus and the hope of Heaven. If you connected with my writing style throughout this book and want to continue the conversation, I think you'll enjoy the Bridget's Cradles podcast that I host, also called *Cradled in Hope*. We release new episodes every month, and there are many wonderful past episodes available for you to listen to as well.

Lastly, if you downloaded the *CIH Guided Journal*, we have a few final journaling prompts for you to complete at the end. These include writing a reflective prayer to God and composing a letter to yourself to open one year from now. We hope these exercises will help you reflect on the journey God has taken you on so far and encourage you to look ahead to where He is leading you.

I trust that God has good plans for you, and I can't wait to see how He uses your life—and your baby's life—for His glory. Keep going, my friend. One foot in front of the other. Jesus is cradling you and your baby every step of the way.

With love, hope, and many prayers,

Ashley

PS—If this book has particularly blessed you or personally led you to Christ, I'd love to hear your testimony. Please share your story at BridgetsCradles.com/ShareYourStory.

Appendix 1

Errors in Our Theology

I grew up in a Christian home, going to church every Sunday and reading parts of my Bible sporadically. In my early twenties, I decided to read the entire Bible from cover to cover for the first time. However, I naively—and selfishly—searched for myself on all the pages.

In every story I read, I sought practical applications that would relate to *my* life and *my* circumstances. I desperately wanted each verse to speak directly *to me*. Have you ever randomly flipped to a page of your Bible, pointed to a verse, and exclaimed that God chose it just for you? I'm glad I'm not the only one!

However, I took a different approach when I reread the Bible chronologically in my thirties. In the decade that had passed since my last full reading of God's Word, I had grown significantly in my spiritual walk with Him. He had helped me through many gut-wrenching trials, and I desired to understand His Word in a deeper way. So, I looked for God—instead of myself—on all the pages of the Bible, and it changed my life.

During that time, I also learned about *hermeneutics*—the way you *interpret* the Bible. There are four different approaches,[1] but I believe in taking a *literal* interpretation from Genesis to Revelation. This means that God says what He means and means what He says.

When we interpret the Bible literally, we don't insert our thoughts or assumptions into our reading. Instead, we seek the plain meaning of what the biblical authors intended when they wrote it based on grammatical and historical context. We do this by asking *"Who, What, When, Where,* and *Why?"* of the author's intentions.

When we need to decipher a passage of text, there are two main interpretation methods: *eisegesis* and *exegesis*. The latter, an *exegetical interpretation* of the text, lends itself to a *literal hermeneutic* of the Bible. But don't let these fancy words confuse you.

The difference between them comes down to a simple question: Are we looking for God in Scripture or are we trying to find ourselves? I've detailed the differences in the chart below.

Bible Interpretation Methods

Eisegesis *Finding Myself in Scripture*	Exegesis *Looking for God in Scripture*
The interpreter *leads into* the text with their own ideas, interpretations, and motives.	The interpreter *draws out* or extracts the meaning from the text.
Desired meaning of the interpreter	Original meaning of the biblical author
—What I think the biblical author meant —What your favorite pastor, influencer, author, podcaster thinks the biblical author meant	What the biblical author meant
What do I want this Scripture to say?	What is God saying in this Scripture?
What Scripture passage fits with the point I want to make?	What does this passage mean?

1. The four major hermeneutic approaches are literal, moral, allegorical, and anagogical.

The difference between these two interpretation methods has serious implications for understanding God and relating His Word to our lives. If we isolate a verse from its surrounding context, we can misconstrue the meaning, leading to a completely different message than the author intended. Unfortunately, we have done this to many verses in the Bible and have developed errors in our theology. When we adopt these flawed beliefs, it can cause us to be confused about who God is and lead us to feel forsaken by Him. These errors in our theology affect our grieving and healing journey more than we realize.

Let me illustrate the significance of interpretation methods using an example from Scripture.

Jeremiah 29:11

"For I know the plans I have for you," declares the Lord, "plans to prosper you and not to harm you, plans to give you hope and a future."

Eisegesis Interpretation | *Finding Myself in Scripture*

God will not cause you harm. Therefore, He will protect you from hardship. He will not allow you to suffer or experience pain. He will bless you and give you the life you've always wanted.

Exegesis Interpretation | *Looking for God in Scripture*

Jeremiah wrote these words to the Jews whom Nebuchadnezzar had carried away into captivity from Jerusalem to Babylon (Jeremiah 29:1).

In the previous chapter, God used Jeremiah to pronounce judgment on the false prophet Hananiah, who lied and told the people they would return home in two years (Jeremiah 28).

God told the people they would live in Babylon for seventy years (Jeremiah 29:10). He encouraged them to build houses, plant gardens, take wives, have children, and seek peace in the city during their captivity (Jeremiah 29:5–7).

He promised the Jews He would bring them back to their land because His thoughts about them are "of peace and not of evil" (Jeremiah 29:11 NKJV).

Summary: Despite their hardship, God sees His people and promises to one day make it right—but in *His* timing and way. In the meantime, He wants them to keep living, building, working, and growing. He will never leave or forsake them. God will be with them in their suffering and struggles.

Do you notice the stark difference between the two and how easily one can fall into the deception of the prosperity gospel? It's no wonder we believe bad things shouldn't happen to good people! So how can we protect ourselves from adopting false beliefs—or correct the ones we've already adopted? The answer is simple: We study and know God's Word. And we stick to an exegetical, literal interpretation of the text.

Appendix 2

The Simple Gospel

• • • CREATION • • •

God created Heaven, earth, and everything on the earth (including animals and humans) in a literal six days. On the seventh day, He rested. God walked alongside the first humans, Adam and Eve, in the Garden of Eden. He desired to have a relationship with His created beings, whom He made in His image. His good and perfect plan was for humans to live forever with Him.

• • • FALL • • •

In the Garden, Adam and Eve (representing all mankind) disobeyed God's command not to eat from the Tree of the Knowledge of Good and Evil. This rejection of God is known as sin, and its consequence is death and eternal separation from Him.

Then, God attempted to restore a relationship with His chosen people, the Jews, through covenants. But the Jews (and humanity in general) continued to disobey God.

God gave the Israelites laws known as the Mosaic Law (which includes the Ten Commandments). Under the Old Covenant, God required the Israelites to make daily animal sacrifices for their sins. However, people kept rejecting His commands and following false gods. There was nothing the Jew or Gentile (non-Jew) could do to reconcile their relationship with God.

• • • REDEMPTION • • •

God sent His one and only Son, Jesus, to be the ultimate sacrifice for humanity's sins. Being God Himself, perfect and sinless, Jesus was the only One who could atone for our sins.

His death and Resurrection fulfilled the New Covenant (which was prophesied in the days of the Old Covenant). His payment for our sins reconciled us to His Father. Those who believe in Him are forgiven and will live eternally in Heaven. This includes babies who went to Heaven before they had a chance to believe.

We are now redeemed, but we still live in a broken world with broken bodies.

• • • RESTORATION • • •

At the coming Resurrection, Jesus will give us glorified immortal bodies. He is coming back and will one day defeat Satan and judge the wicked. Death and evil will be no more. We will live forever with Him on the New Earth, also known as the New Heaven. Creation will be restored to its Eden state.

Appendix 3

The Disciples' Testimony

His Disciples . . .	Scripture Support
Observed Jesus perform miracles, such as:	
1. Turning water into wine	1. John 2:1–11
2. Walking on water	2. Matthew 14:22–33
3. Casting out demons	3. Mark 1:23–28; Matthew 8:28–34; Matthew 12:22; Matthew 15:22–28; Matthew 17:14–21
4. Healing the sick, leper, lame, paralytic, blind, and deaf	4. Mark 1:40–45; Matthew 8:5–13; Matthew 9:1–8; Luke 8:43–48; Matthew 9:27–33; John 5:1–9; Mark 1:30–31; Mark 7:31–37; Mark 8:22–26; John 9:1–38; Luke 17:11–19
5. Raising the dead	5. Luke 7:11–18; Matthew 9:18–26; John 11:1–46
6. Calming a storm	6. Matthew 8:23–27
7. Feeding 5,000+ people with five loaves of bread and two fish	7. Matthew 14:15–21

*This is not an exhaustive list.

His Disciples . . .	Scripture Support
Performed miracles themselves (by the power and authority given to them by Jesus)	
• Peter walked on water	• Matthew 14:28–31
• Cast out demons and healed people	• Matthew 10:7–8; Mark 6:12–13; Luke 9:10; Luke 10:1–17
• Raised people from the dead	• Acts 9:36–43; Acts 20:9–12
John watched Jesus being crucified (The other disciples fled; also present at Jesus' crucifixion were Mary, Jesus' mother, her sister, Mary the wife of Clopas, and Mary Magdalene.)	Matthew 26:56; John 19:25–27
Saw Jesus' glorified body after His Resurrection	Matthew 28:16–20; Luke 24:13–49; John 20:19–29
Witnessed Jesus' Ascension into Heaven	Acts 1:1–11

Appendix 4

Crowns in Heaven

Christians will receive Heavenly rewards for their service to Christ. There are five different crowns described by the authors of the New Testament.

Heavenly Crown	Biblical Reference	Who will get it?
The Imperishable or Incorruptible Crown	1 Corinthians 9:24–25	Paul contrasts this crown with earthly crowns that "will not last." This crown is for those who run their race with self-discipline and perseverance for the Kingdom.
The Crown of Rejoicing	1 Thessalonians 2:19	Paul mentions this crown after evangelizing the Thessalonians. This crown is for those who win souls for Christ.
The Crown of Righteousness	2 Timothy 4:8	Paul mentions he will receive this crown for fighting the good fight, finishing the race, and keeping the faith. He also mentions this crown is for those who look forward to Jesus' return.
The Crown of Glory	1 Peter 5:4	Peter mentions this crown when addressing elders and shepherds of God's flock. This crown is for those who serve and watch over the Church.
The Crown of Life	James 1:12; Revelation 2:10	John mentions this crown when addressing the Church of Smyrna. This crown is for those who suffer persecution for Christ, even to the point of death. This crown is sometimes known as the Martyr's Crown.

Grieving mothers could receive four or even all five of the Heavenly crowns.[1] However, we will not receive the crowns *just because* we lost a baby. Instead, we will receive them because of *how we responded* to losing a baby. Our grief gives us the opportunity to earn crowns in Heaven. If we run our race for Christ, fight the good fight, and use our grief for His glory, we will receive Heavenly crowns!

1. I adhere to a complementarian biblical view that pastor and elder positions in the Church should only be held by men, as outlined by Paul in 1 Timothy 3:1-7 and Titus 1:5-9. Women can and should serve in the Church and ministry, even in leadership positions, but not as pastors or elders. It is unclear whether the Crown of Glory is reserved for pastors and elders only or for all Church and ministry leaders. In the latter case, it would be possible for a woman to receive the Crown of Glory. Lastly, the Crown of Life is a high honor reserved for those who are persecuted or killed for their faith.

Acknowledgments

To my husband, Matt—Losing Bridget in our first year of marriage was difficult, but God used her life to bring us closer to Him and to each other. Thank you for the countless ways you've supported me and Bridget's Cradles over the years. Nothing I've done, including this book, would be possible without you. *Cradled in Hope* is an extension of our ministry together and did not come without sacrifice on your part. You took great care of our boys while I was on several weekend writing trips and during many Saturday writing sessions leading up to my manuscript deadline. You are an amazing Daddy! I am blessed to be married to such a good, faithful, handsome man. I love you, Matt.

To my sons, Branton and Brenner—I thank God every day for choosing me to be your Mommy. You are both so smart, sweet, and silly. Knowing each of your unique personalities has only made me more excited to meet your sister in Heaven. It warms my heart how much you love Bridget and how you include her in our conversations and prayers. Visiting her grave, celebrating her Heaven Day, and coming with me to Bridget's Cradles HQ has been a normal part of your childhood. I pray that her life has only made Heaven and God more real to you. My greatest desire for each of you is that you would follow Jesus all the days of your life. I long to spend eternity as a family in Heaven. I will love you both forever!

To my mom, Teresa—This book, and Bridget's Cradles, wouldn't exist without you. Your love as a mother and grandmother prompted you to knit Bridget's mint green cradle. Only God knew then how impactful that small gesture would be. Hundreds of thousands of grieving mothers have been comforted by what you started, but perhaps no one more than me. This ministry has given me purpose in my pain and changed my life forever. I am eternally indebted to God for blessing me with such a loving and thoughtful mom. You are the most amazing "Grammy" and "Gigi" to my three children. I look forward to making more memories with you on earth as you await the most glorious reunion with SRG and Bridget in Heaven.

To my siblings, Tara and Aaron—We share a beautiful childhood together and so many wonderful memories. Having a sibling is truly like having a forever friend. But also, in your case, being my sibling means being a forever Bridget's Cradles *Wave of Light* volunteer. Thank you for always supporting your niece's ministry and for participating in her Heavenly birthday parties every year. You are some of the few people who were able to hold her, and I appreciate you remembering her with us. I love you both with all my heart.

To my in-laws, Rod and Susan—Thank you for your prayers and support during my book-writing journey and through all my years of balancing motherhood and ministry. I am thankful to have Christian in-laws who love and care for our boys on earth *and* our daughter in Heaven. Thank you for always honoring Bridget in your family and for the many ways you support the ministry. Susan—you are an incredible mother-in-law and

Nana. I appreciate you playing with the boys and allowing me time to work and write. I wouldn't be able to do everything I do without you.

To my friend, Amanda Farris—Although we've always lived states apart, you're one of my closest friends and one of the most selfless people I know. You left a paid career to volunteer full-time with Bridget's Cradles in 2016 and currently serve as our director of communications and marketing. Your eye for design, understanding of CRM software systems, and willingness to perform tedious administrative tasks have propelled Bridget's Cradles to where it is today. Thank you for your encouragement and motivation on my writing journey. From the pep talks on my basement couch to sending me writing care packages, you have always supported me! I am also grateful for your beautiful design work on the *CIH Guided Journal*.

To my friend, Casey Siegrist—Who knew a friendship could form in a cemetery? Though I wish we could have met another way, God had a plan for our children, Jack and Bridget, to be buried beside each other. You were my first bereaved mom friend, and we walked through all our "firsts" together—the holidays, our due dates, and Heaven Days. I'll always remember telling you about my dream of starting Bridget's Cradles while we sat in her empty nursery. You said you wanted to do it with me, and you've served with me in the ministry ever since. My life wouldn't be the same without your loyal friendship, and Bridget's Cradles wouldn't be what it is without your precious Jack.

To my friend, Kelcey Crone—You are my person, and I am yours. God connected us after you received one of our cradles for your son, David. We forged a deep friendship through our mutual love for Jesus and His Word. Your testimony is powerful, and Jesus shines through you. I love watching Him work in your life.

You always say that after David went to Heaven, you "came to Bridget's Cradles and never left." I hope you never do because serving with you in ministry is my absolute favorite.

To my literary agent, Blythe Daniel—Thank you for believing in me and the message of *Cradled in Hope*. In a publishing world often focused on an author's platform size, you were more concerned with my character and the Kingdom potential of my book. I am grateful to have found a wise and discerning literary agent who is now a dear friend and sister in Christ. Thank you for your thoughtful edits to my book proposal and your patience in presenting it to publishers. As I navigated my son's newborn days and subsequent health issues, which delayed the process, you reminded me that it would happen in God's timing. You were right, and I loved celebrating my book deal with you over dinner in Colorado Springs. Thank you for being a fierce prayer warrior for me and this book.

To my acquisitions editor, Jennifer Dukes Lee—When Blythe presented my book proposal to publishing houses, she mentioned that it might be difficult for a first-time author like me to attract the attention of a prestigious publisher like Bethany House. I will always remember the day she forwarded your publishing offer to my inbox. After years of dreaming of a book deal, there you were, believing in me and wanting to publish my book! I cried tears of joy that day and have felt immensely blessed working with you ever since. Your insightful feedback and words of encouragement have made *Cradled in Hope* everything God intended it to be. I appreciate that you gave me the creative freedom—and word count—to share everything the Holy Spirit placed on my heart. Through this journey, you have become a trusted friend. I will always treasure my time with you at Glen Eyrie. Thank you for "leaving the light on for me."

To my team at Bethany House—You are the dream team and the real deal. You are much more than just a publishing house— you are truly brothers and sisters in Christ. You comforted me when my dad was in the hospital, sent flowers after he went to Heaven, defended me against spiritual attacks, and walked with me through one of the hardest seasons of my life leading up to my book launch. Working with you has been the honor of my life.

Stephanie Smith—Thank you for embracing my vision for the title and subtitle. I appreciated our collaborative effort in creating the secondary subtitle, which was your brilliant suggestion. I am thrilled with how it turned out, as it perfectly encapsulates the message of my book.

Dan Pitts—You brought my vision to life and designed the best possible cover. It is warm, inviting, and comforting—everything I hoped that it would be for the grieving mothers who will read it.

Sharon Hodge—You were a delight to work with and an incredible editor. Your final revisions polished my manuscript and gave me confidence it was ready to print.

To the many more at Bethany House and Baker Publishing Group—Thank you, from the bottom of my heart, for publishing *Cradled in Hope* and for helping get it into the hands of grieving mothers near and far.

To my peer-editing team, Abby Norton, Casey Siegrist, Cristian Deluera, Edith Boyle, Kelcey Crone, Mary Brewer, and Rebekah Beresford—Having a peer-editing team isn't a requirement for publishing a book. Yet, I felt convicted to have seven sisters in Christ— five of whom are bereaved moms—read my manuscript before anyone else. Ladies, I am incredibly grateful for your commitment to providing valuable feedback and constructive commentary. Your experience with pain, unwavering love for the Lord, biblical wisdom, and a keen eye for detail undoubtedly enhanced my revisions. I am confident that *Cradled in Hope* is better because of you.

To my support group leadership team, Casey Siegrist, Kelcey Crone, and Dena Broderick—You have been with me on this journey since the very beginning. Over the past seven years, you have repeatedly heard me share the message of this book in our support groups. You offered your own stories and insight, which helped shape my book. I love serving with you in the Little Blue Barn—or as we call it, KQ, for Kechi Quarters—in memory of your sons, Jack Monroe (Casey), David Bruce (Kelcey), and Gabriel Mason (Dena). We have shared many tears, laughs, memories, and inside jokes. I will always treasure my days—and late nights—at KQ with you. I am forever grateful for your friendship and service in ministry.

To every Bridget's Cradles volunteer—You are the hands and feet of Jesus. We couldn't do what we do without you. Thank you for each beautiful cradle you knit, crochet, or sew. Each one holds God's most precious creation and points grieving families to the hope of the Gospel. You are doing Kingdom work. We are blessed to have you on our team.

To you, my grieving mom friend—This was all for you. From October 2023 to January 2025, I burned through eight candles and spent over 500 hours typing these words for you. Many days, I wanted to give up and doubted myself as an author. But *you* kept me going. I imagined my book in your hands and envisioned you drawing near to Jesus because of something I wrote. I pressed on, knowing the God who asked me to share this message with you holds the power to heal your broken heart. I am grateful He connected us through my book. Whether I meet you one day in person, some evening on Hope Online, or eventually in Heaven, know I love and care for you deeply. Thank you for entrusting me to be on this journey with you.

Notes

Chapter 1 Sitting with Jesus

1. This quote is most often attributed to Chaplain Robert Orr (Kindred Hospice).

2. This quote is attributed to Jamie Anderson.

3. Lori Stanley Roeleveld, "What Does it Mean to Lament? Bible Meaning Explained," Crosswalk.com, May 9, 2024, https://www.crosswalk.com/faith/bible-study/what-is-a-lament-in-the-bible.html.

4. Anonymous. This is posted widely on the internet, but not with a name attached to it.

Chapter 2 Broken and Bleeding

1. R. C. Sproul Jr., quoted in Clay Jones, *Why Does God Allow Evil: Compelling Answers for Life's Toughest Questions* (Eugene, OR: Harvest House, 2017), 77.

2. *A Grief Observed* by C. S. Lewis © copyright 1961 CS Lewis Pte Ltd. Extract used with permission.

3. Elizabeth Urbanowicz, "How to Help Kids Discern the True Gospel from a False Gospel," *Foundation Worldview*, January 5, 2022, https://foundationworldview.com/blog/the-false-gospel-how-to-help-kids-discern-the-true-gospel.

4. Helen H. Lemmel, "Turn Your Eyes upon Jesus," copyright 1922 by Singspiration Music/ASCAP. All rights reserved.

5. Lemmel, "Turn Your Eyes upon Jesus."

Chapter 3 The Gospel Changes Everything

1. Paraphrased from Charles Spurgeon, "The sovereignty of God is the pillow on which the Christian lays his head," quoted in Ernest Easley, *Resting in God's Sovereignty: A 30-Day Devotional on God's Plan for His People* (Brentwood, TN: B&H, 2024), 1.

2. Although the quoted stanza is included in John Newton's "Amazing Grace" in many hymnals in the United States, it was not written by Newton and did not appear in the "Amazing Grace" originally published in *Olney Hymns* in 1779. This verse appeared at the end of "Jerusalem, My Happy Home" in *A Collection of Sacred Ballads* (1790) and later was appended to versions of "Amazing Grace" in hymnals in 1909 and 1910, according to *Hymnology Archive,* https://www.hymnologyarchive.com/amazing-grace.

Chapter 4 A Firm Foundation

1. "Best-Selling Book," *Guinness World Records,* https://www.guinnessworldrecords.com/world-records/best-selling-book-of-non-fiction.
2. Daniel Radosh, "The Good Book Business," *The New Yorker,* December 10, 2006, https://www.newyorker.com/magazine/2006/12/18/the-good-book-business.
3. "Best-Selling Book," *Guinness.*
4. *Mere Christianity* by CS Lewis © copyright 1942, 1943, 1944, 1952 CS Lewis Pte Ltd.
5. "Apologetics," *Britannica,* December 6, 2024, https://www.britannica.com/topic/apologetics.
6. "How Did the Apostle Paul Die?" *Got Questions,* accessed January 3, 2024, https://www.gotquestions.org/how-did-Paul-die.html.
7. "How Did the Apostle Peter Die?" *Got Questions,* accessed May 22, 2024. https://www.gotquestions.org/apostle-Peter-die.html.
8. "Worldviews: The Questions We Ask and the Stories We Live," Impact 360 Institute, accessed May 22, 2024, https://www.impact360institute.org/articles/worldviews-the-questions-we-ask-and-the-stories-we-live/.
9. Edward Mote, "My Hope Is Built on Nothing Less," 1834, Hymnary, accessed May 22, 2024, https://hymnary.org/text/my_hope_is_built_on_nothing_less.

Chapter 5 Heaven on Earth

1. Randy C. Alcorn, "What We Assume about Heaven" (abbreviated) chart, in *Heaven* (Tyndale House, 2004), 161.

Chapter 6 For He Is Good

1. A.W. Tozer, *The Knowledge of the Holy: The Attributes of God, Their Meaning in the Christian Life* (Lutterworth, 2022), 1.
2. Alyssa Roat, "What Is Agape Love?," Christianity.com, April 17, 2024, https://www.christianity.com/wiki/christian-terms/what-does-agape-love-really-mean-in-the-bible.html.

Chapter 7 Grace upon Grace

1. You can read more at Bible Hub's *Strong's Concordance*: *cakak*, Strong's 5526, which can be found at https://biblehub.com/hebrew/5526.htm, and *sakak* at Strong's 5526b.

2. Alfred Lord Tennyson, "In Memoriam" (Knight & Millet, London: 1850), 102.

Chapter 8 They Know Not What They Do

1. Gary Chapman, "What Are the 5 Love Languages?" *Love Languages*, https://5lovelanguages.com/learn.

Chapter 9 The Good Fight

1. A Google image search of "God's Voice vs. Satan's Voice" will return dozens of various charts that are similar. I created my own summary chart, but the specific nature of the comparisons within the chart or its cells means there is potentially some overlap in content among charts.

Chapter 10 A Renewed Mind

1. Dictionary.com, "trigger," accessed May 22, 2024, https://www.dictionary.com/browse/trigger.

2. Traci Pedersen, "All About Amygdala Hijack," *Pysch Central,* October 14, 2021, https://psychcentral.com/health/amygdala-hijack.

3. Olivia Guy-Evans, "Amygdala: What It Is & Its Functions," *Simply Psychology*, December 14, 2023, https://www.simplypsychology.org/amygdala.html.

4. Guy-Evans, "Amygdala: What It Is."

5. Pedersen, "Amygdala Hijack."

6. Pedersen, "Amygdala Hijack."

7. Pedersen, "Amygdala Hijack."

8. Todd Thatcher, "Can Emotional Trauma Cause Brain Damage?" Highland Springs Specialty Clinic, February 4, 2019, https://highlandspringsclinic.org/can-emotional-trauma-cause-brain-damage/.

9. "Grounding Techniques," University of Prince Edward Island, accessed May 22, 2024, https://files.upei.ca/vpaf/svpro/grounding_techniques_peirsac.pdf.

10. Pedersen, "Amygdala Hijack."

Chapter 12 More Than Gold

1. Ashley Opliger, "Declaration of Faith," a statement read at the opening of Bridget's Cradles support groups.

Chapter 13 With the Same Comfort

1. *Mere Christianity* by CS Lewis © copyright 1942, 1943, 1944, 1952 CS Lewis Pte Ltd.

2. Brett Meador shared this message in a sermon titled "The Power of Prayer and Praise," Athey Creek Church, February 9, 2025, YouTube, 1:05:32, https://www.youtube.com/watch?v=AffJT4okzrU.

Chapter 14 Our Future Forever

1. "What Is the Protoevangelium?," *Got Questions*, accessed February 17, 2025, https://www.gotquestions.org/protoevangelium.html.

2. "What Does Maranatha Mean?," *Got Questions*, accessed May 22, 2024, https://www.gotquestions.org/maranatha.html.

3. Horatio G. Spafford, "It Is Well with My Soul," 1873. Public domain.

4. Randy Peterson, *Be Still My Soul: The Inspiring Stories Behind 175 of the Most-Loved Hymns* (Tyndale House, 2014), 153.

5. "Horatio Spafford," Wikipedia, accessed May 22, 2024, https://en.wikipedia.org/wiki/Horatio_Spafford.

6. Charles Spurgeon, "10 Spurgeon Quotes on Dying Well," The Spurgeon Center for Biblical Preaching at Midwestern Seminary, June 29, 2017, accessed May 22, 2024, https://www.spurgeon.org/resource-library/blog-entries/10-spurgeon-quotes-on-dying-well/.

Ashley Opliger is the founder and executive director of Bridget's Cradles. After her daughter, Bridget, was stillborn at twenty-four weeks, she left her career as a speech-language pathologist to start the ministry in her daughter's empty nursery. Under Ashley's leadership, Bridget's Cradles now donates thousands of knit and crocheted cradles to over 1,500 hospitals in all fifty states from their headquarters near Wichita, Kansas.

Jeanize Cilliers Photography

Ashley hosts the *Cradled in Hope* podcast and leads support groups for grieving moms. She is married to Matt, and they have three children: a daughter in Heaven and two sons on earth. She loves Jesus and desires to share the hope of Heaven with families grieving the loss of a baby.

Ministry and motherhood keep Ashley very busy, but in her spare time, she enjoys making memories with family and friends, going on long walks outside, lifting weights, and traveling. After her boys go to bed, if she's not doing the dishes or spending time with Matt, she can be found stargazing in their hot tub, playing her electric drums, journaling, studying the Bible, or reading a Christian nonfiction book.

Connect with Ashley:

AshleyOpliger.com   /AshleyOpliger   @AshleyOpliger

Connect with Bridget's Cradles:

BridgetsCradles.com   /BridgetsCradles  @BridgetsCradles

Cradled *in* Hope
Guided Journal

DOWNLOAD YOUR
(FREE) JOURNAL

√ Prayer, Scripture, and reflection questions
√ Space for journaling and taking notes
√ Encouragement and healing steps

YOU'LL ALSO RECEIVE BRIDGET'S CRADLES FREE E-BOOK
"MEMORIAL IDEAS FOR A BABY IN HEAVEN."

Longing for Heaven?
Want to share your hope with others?

Visit BridgetsCradles.com/Shop to browse our apparel collection for grieving moms, featuring our signature *HEAVEN IS MY HOPE* design and many others. Your purchase will benefit the mission of Bridget's Cradles and provide cradles and hope-filled resources to bereaved families across the country.

Bridget's Cradles

Cradled in Hope
podcast

**Cradled in Hope
Podcast**

Hope-Filled Episodes for Moms Grieving a Baby in Heaven

Join host Ashley as she interviews grieving parents who share their story along with practical wisdom.

Each Gospel-focused episode moves listeners from heartbreak to hope and pain to purpose.

listen and be encouraged:

 BRIDGETSCRADLES.COM**/PODCAST**

Available on Spotify, Apple Podcasts, or Anywhere You Podcast

Bridget's Cradles

Hope Online
support group

Join us for a monthly Christ-centered support group for moms who have lost a baby.

Together, we focus on finding hope and healing with Jesus in community with each other.

find support

register now:

BRIDGETSCRADLES.COM/**HOPEONLINE**